ANNUALS & BEDDING PLANTS

ANNUALS & BEDDING PLANTS

NIGEL COLBORN

CONRAN OCTOPUS

First published in Great Britain in 1994 by
Conran Octopus Limited
37 Shelton Street
London WC2H 9HN

Reprinted 1994, 1995

British Library Cataloguing-in-Publication-Data
A catalogue record for this book is available from the British Library.

ISBN 1 85029 547 6

Special projects photographed by **Clive Nichols**
Illustrations by **Liz Pepperell**

Senior Editor: **Sarah Pearce**
Art Editor: **Sue Storey**
Designer: **Sally Powell**
Picture Research: **Christine Rista**
Text Editor: **Jackie Matthews**
Editorial Assistant: **Charlotte Coleman-Smith**
Production: **Julia Golding**

Typeset by Dorchester Typesetting Group Ltd
Printed and bound in Hong Kong

Index by Indexing Specialists, Hove, East Sussex

RIGHT *Pelargonium* 'Orbit Glow' (zonal) with *Lobelia erinus*.

Contents

SETTING THE PREMISE

If you think that bedding is limited to massed flowers arranged in garish displays, think again. Looked at as a particular technique of grouping interesting species in exciting combinations, bedding presents a wealth of opportunities to be seized on and exploited as part of the artistic – and the artful – gardener's creative process. Planting is, after all, no more nor less than a means of decorating an area with a selection of colours and textures to create a desired result. Different combinations result in different  moods and styles, and bedding, more than with any other planting system, has the ability to produce displays with maximum impact.

LEFT *Bedding can be a splash of colour in the garden – a sort of gardener's garnish. Here an otherwise dull spot beneath trees is brought to life with a spring splash of golden doronicums (leopard's bane).*

ABOVE *A stone trough displays a stunning colour partnership: glowing winter-flowering pansies with hyacinths to match.*

What is Bedding?

Bedding is often thought of as temporary, formal, brightly coloured and sometimes fussy. It certainly can be all of these but, just as easily, it can be restful, informal, arranged in soft colours or even shades of simple green. Bedding schemes can be used as low key, background planting. They can be long term – the base of a hedge furnished with a simple line of hostas, for instance. Or they can be planned for maximum impact, packed with fiery colours and exciting contrasts of texture. Bedding has as much artistic potential as any other kind of creative planting and should never be simply dismissed as the 'canned music' of gardening.

The fashion for bedding evolved during the nineteenth century and is still widely practised in public gardens all over the world in its traditional form. Plants used vary hugely, of course, according to climate and local preferences, but the patterns and styles are surprisingly uniform. Thus, a red scheme with dark foliage in the tropics, effected with poinsettias and cannas, could look exactly the same in a cold country, where the beds are planted with dahlias and salvias.

In a private garden, the concept of bedding has the potential to embrace much more than this narrow style. And if we analyse the technique itself, we can see how the principles of bedding can be applied to a diversity of planting opportunities.

The main feature of bedding is massing: that is, numbers of the same plants used together, with the effect of creating a uniform, or near uniform, texture. In traditional bedding schemes, different plants are massed together to create formal patterns. Scaled down in size and scope to suit small areas, this nineteenth-century style is still useful for creating short-term displays, even in a tiny garden. Parts of the garden which are glanced at fleetingly, rather than lingered in, and where bright displays can present an exciting highlight, make first class candidates for flowerbeds of this kind.

Geometric shapes planted with short-term displays are but one aspect of bedding, however, for the concept can be stretched much further. Permanent or at least medium-term plants can be used; foliage can provide a restful visual alternative to flowers; planting

positions and styles can be varied, with dense massing for drama or sparser coverings for more subtle effects.

ROTATING THE DISPLAY

Although most bedding is temporary, an element of continuity is easy to achieve by replanting. In the nineteenth century it was common practice to prepare different displays each season, but the labour involved was truly immense. Nowadays, two shows per year is more practical. A conventional timetable would be to plant in autumn for the spring display, and to plant out the main display of summer bedding as soon as the risk of frost has passed. There are many other options, however, which need not involve a great deal of labour, although, from a practical point of view, you may find you have to strip out one season's bedding before it has finished flowering, simply to get the next planted up in time. An example might be a late-summer display of chrysanthemums, followed by some late-flowering spring bulbs.

Permanent bedding plants, such as lavender or roses, can span several seasons, providing flower in one period, foliage in another. Where space is restricted, bedding schemes can also be set up in containers or raised beds.

LEFT *The pansy 'The Joker' with midseason hybrid tulips. Spring bedding is usually planted in autumn, replacing the worn-out summer display. Winter-flowering pansies will throw sporadic blooms all winter, until they join the tulips in spring with a final flourish of colour.*

OPPOSITE *Clipped box hedges are a traditional way to create formal enclosures – here,* Sedum spectabile *and* nicotianas.

BELOW Antirrhinums, *Phlox* drummondii *and African marigolds blend exciting colours together to lead the way to the front door.*

TYPES OF BEDDING SCHEME

Here are a few specific examples of how bedding can be made to work in a variety of different garden settings.

Traditional A narrow bed or border, perhaps no more than 2m (6ft) deep and 6m (20ft) wide and running along the front or back of a house, or along a wall, could be an ideal setting for a classic bedding scheme. Limited space would prohibit too fussy an arrangement but there would still be plenty of scope for tight groupings of two, three or perhaps at

most four kinds of plant. Of these, two – scarlet pelargoniums, perhaps, and bright blue petunias – could display contrasting flower colours, while the rest – silver senecio, say, or dark-leaved amaranthus – could provide a foliage background.

Where beds are divided by a central path leading to another part of the garden, it would be natural to create replicating beds on either side. Within low clipped hedges of box, rosemary or lavender, you could ring the changes, choosing sometimes hot, strong colours, and at other times cool, soothing blues or pale pinks and silver foliage. Thus, bedded salvias, commonplace though they may be, will provide a burning drama, whereas a thick planting of silvery blue pansies will shimmer like the surface of a lake.

Highlights A garden where, for the sake of saving labour, there is little more than grass and trees or shrubs can look rather dreary in certain seasons. A simple border of bedding, thoughtfully positioned to highlight a dull spot or to divide one part off from another, enables the gardener to add interest, not only as a result of simply dividing the space, but also by making the division itself a centre of attraction. Take a dozen lily bulbs, for example, and place these in a group between shrubs in grass, and the resulting burst of colour and fragrance will give many weeks of delight. Alternatively, among all the informality of a mixed planting, try setting up a small, symmetrical bed and plant it with a single species – pale pink impatiens, perhaps – and the result is a small focal point which makes a striking contrast with the rest.

Change of texture With care, bedding can be gently incorporated into even the most expertly devised permanent planting schemes

with gratifying results. For example, a mixed border designed to provide maximum interest in high summer can look drab in spring when the perennials are no more than tantalizing tufts of foliage. Plant the whole liberally with tulips and the bed is transformed into a dramatic, albeit short-lived, display for the spring period that is wholly different in character from the more permanent style. Moreover, when the tulips have finished flowering, they will die back to nothing with amazing speed, or they can be removed, making way for their more sedate border companions.

Furnishing shrubs Shrubs are wonderful at their best but, apart from a handful of exceptions, can look rather boring during their 'off' season. One solution to this is to underplant them with permanent ground cover. But that, too, can sometimes be as boring as the quiescent shrubs themselves. A mix of bedding and ground cover, however, or a carefully selected group of bedding plants on their own, can help to shift the emphasis away from the shrubs down to nearer ground level. Winter-flowering evergreens, for example, could be underplanted with direct-sown *Limnanthes douglasii*. These little plants self-seed profusely, forming a bright emerald carpet in early spring that is followed by a splash of brilliant white-and-gold flowers which eventually fade and seed ready for next season.

Contained bedding Containers can be used in so many different ways that, as far as bedding is concerned, they alone can provide enough subject matter for books in themselves. Their versatile nature enables you to ring the changes as often as you like, not only by replanting them, but by moving them around or re-arranging them as their flowering display changes.

Although some containers are more often used for permanent planting, the great majority are replanted at least once a season with temporary bedding displays. Besides the usual pots, urns, troughs and less conventional planters – all of which offer a whole range of planting opportunities – there are window boxes and hanging baskets. Such dependable and long-flowering bedding plants as trailing lobelia, fuchsias and pelargoniums of all kinds flower every year in literally millions of hanging baskets all around the world.

Where space is limited, containers might be the only way that bedding plants can be displayed to greatest advantage in the garden. Grouping the pots and tubs together into carefully co-ordinated displays minimizes 'bittiness' and creates focal points of dense visual interest. Indeed, this is really not very different from any other form of bedding technique, that is, the practice of massing plants of similar kinds together to make a composition that is a great deal more than the sum of its parts.

LEFT *Bedding can be used to fill an empty space quickly. On this small square of soil, a group of* Nicotiana *'Domino Salmon Pink', pansies in soft shades, and a clump of perennial cranesbills merge to create colourful ground cover for summer.*

OPPOSITE *Sweet williams, raised from seed and planted in bold groups, make a strong splash of colour at the base of an old wall. Their colours are clean and bright, and their old-world style harmonizes well with the climbing roses.*

Potted Bedding

Aspect and conditions: A well-lit, sheltered, south-facing site with protecting walls on all sides. A soil-less compost was used for all plants, with, in some cases, extra sand and a little loam added.

ABOVE Lobelia erinus *is the species from which many garden cultivars derive. It has larger flowers and a spreading habit.*

Scheme: A collection of ten containers, varying in size from a huge water tank to a small alpine pan, was assembled to form a group. The objective was to create a harmonious planting, even though the containers themselves made a disparate group.

A vigorous trailing species of lobelia was used in most of the planters, and served to pull the scheme together by providing a common theme to all the pots. The pelargonium 'Paton's Unique', with its emerald foliage and cerise flowers, made the centrepiece of the colour scheme, which veered towards blue at one end and yellow at the other. A bowl of tiny yellow violas were moved in when in flower.

Results: The lobelia did more than a token binding. It proved to be so vigorous that it intertwined through the planting, hiding the containers and making a continuous bank of vegetation. This may not have suited some tastes, especially if the containers were particularly beautiful, but as an ensemble this planting brightened the corner of an otherwise humdrum courtyard and retained its colour all summer.

Plants used:

1 *Pelargonium* Fragrans Group
2 *Argyranthemum frutescens* unnamed single pink
3 *Lobelia erinus*
4 *Eriobotrya japonica*
5 *Convolvulus sabatius*
6 *Pelargonium* 'Paton's Unique'
7 *Argyranthemum frutescens* unnamed double primrose yellow
8 *Viola* 'Sunbeam'

What is a Bedding Plant?

Having broadened the concept of the bedding technique, the next step is to be able to evaluate appropriate plants. To perform well, each variety must exhibit as many as possible of the special qualities listed here.

Good association The most important quality of a bedding plant is an ability to look attractive when grown together with other plants of its own kind. Species which colonize naturally in the wild are obvious candidates for most kinds of bedding. Crowded in a border, they are closer to their natural state than are the 'loners' of the plant world.

Good bedding also needs to fit comfortably into a background of companion plants, whether this be made up of other bedding or more diverse planting.

Strength of character Bedding plants should be showy without shouting aloud their presence. Colours must contrast or harmonize readily with any foliage making a natural backing. Growth habits should enable the plants to merge or grow together without leaving awkward gaps.

One criticism often levelled at traditional bedding schemes is that they offer little opportunity to enjoy the plants as individuals. This view is, however, a specious one. The evening scent of nicotianas and the subtle changes in the hue of tulip petals as they age are but two of the many examples of how

LEFT *Bedding can be used to highlight the dividing point between two parts of a garden. The impact of this vivid display of polyanthus and wallflowers at a gap in the wall will be heightened further by their sweet fragrance.*

interesting individuals comprise the whole. Looking at bedding is a little like studying a regiment of guards performing a military drill. The overall spectacle is one of colourful automata, but as the soldiers march past, you begin to distinguish their features and recognize them as individuals.

Sustained displays Plants which flower early and continue in full colour – come rain or shine – until frost begins, make the most desirable bedding subjects. The overriding quality of such time-honoured genera as pelargoniums, fuchsias and French marigolds is that they do not stop flowering and are, therefore, ideal bedding plants.

In our quest for imaginative and original bedding, it is possible to add a further, exciting range to these basic plants, for such perennials as potentillas, penstemons and many of the world's hardy geraniums or cranesbills all have the potential to make model bedding alternatives.

Clean colour, bright foliage Bedding should supply the garden with a steady and reliable source of colour and texture. Colours need to be clean and clear if they are to contrast or harmonize with each other effectively. Foliage plants must be able to stay bright and fresh, even when under stress.

Happy to be transplanted Whether raised from seed or propagated by cuttings, bedding plants should be easy to transplant and must establish themselves in their new sites without fuss. It should even be possible, with some plants, to ring the changes *during* the display season, perhaps introducing new plants when they are in full bloom.

LEFT *With its elegant blooms, gleaming foliage and very long flowering season, the pelargonium is a model bedding plant.*

BELOW *Bedding often consists of large numbers of plants, arranged to create blocks or bands of colour. Close to, the individual characteristics of the plants become obvious.*

HARDY ANNUALS

Malcolmia maritima
(Virginian Stock)
An unremarkable plant,
being only 20cm (8in) in
height, but it will flower
within four weeks of sowing
and, if massed, can be
endearing with its multi-
coloured flowers. In the
event of a crop failure or
in lieu of something more
special, this may be all
you can grow!

Papaver rhoeas
Hardy annuals which
develop speedily from seed,
and flower in a wide range
of colours. The Shirley
strain, developed by the
Reverend Wilks in the late
nineteenth century, comes
in lemon, strawberry and
candy pink shades. 'Mother
of Pearl' is a sumptuous
blend of silken maroons,
dusky pinks and near whites
with dove grey pollen.

Tropaeolum majus
Glorious warm colours on
vigorous creeping plants
which will rapidly cover the
ground. The variety 'Alaska'
has variegated foliage and
creeps less invasively than
some forms. Young leaves
and flowers can be used to
spice up salads; the pickled
seeds make interesting
substitutes for capers.

CLASSIFICATION OF BEDDING PLANTS

Almost any type of plant can be used for bedding, but in practice the bulk of the bedding
repertoire comes from annuals, or plants
treated as annuals. The following are the
major classifications that you are most
likely to encounter on seed packets and in
planting recommendations.

Hardy Annual These are plants that complete
their lifecycle of growing, flowering and setting seed within one year. They are fully frost
hardy, so can be reared from seed sown outside. They are only normally available as
seeds. Whole bedding schemes can be direct-
sown using hardy annuals, with none of the
labour associated with indoor-sown plants.
Examples of suitable hardy annuals are cornflowers, calendulas and larkspurs.

Half-Hardy Annual These are, technically,
annuals that cannot be raised outdoors in
regions where there is winter frost. Their
mode of production is therefore winter or
spring sowing under protection, usually a
greenhouse, where they are kept until after
the risk of frost is minimal. French marigolds,
Phlox drummondii and nemesias are examples
of half-hardy annuals.

In practice, many plants sold as half-hardy
annuals would be perennial in warmer climates, and this group includes some of our
most successful bedding plants, such as petunias, nicotianas, verbenas and lobelia. In these
cases, the designation half-hardy annual refers
to the way the plants are grown in northern
climates: they are sown under protection,
planted out for the summer, then stripped
out and discarded after flowering. HHAs provide some of the longest-flowering and most
reliable of all bedding plants.

True annuals die after seeding, but perennials grown as half-hardy annuals can be propagated vegetatively. Cuttings of good varieties
can be taken in quantity during the summer,
and grown on under winter protection to
make strong young plants for bedding out the
following year.

Hardy Biennial These plants need two growing seasons in which to develop to flowering
stage: they produce leaves in the first season,
flowers in the next; then the plant seeds and
dies. Several popular spring-flowering bedding
plants, such as wallflowers, are biennials.
Their seed is sown outdoors in nursery beds in
midsummer, and transplanted in autumn.

Tender Perennial These are plants that will
continue to grow and flower over many years,
provided they are in a frost-free environment.
Such a definition technically extends to some
of those plants listed above as half-hardy
annuals (verbenas, lobelia etc.), but in practice the term is used to refer to those plants
that are overwintered under protection and
either replanted the following year as the
'framework' plants within a scheme, or used
as 'stock' plants for producing cuttings. Examples of tender perennials are pelargoniums,
argyranthemums, fuchsias, osteospermums
and *Cosmos atrosanguineus*.

Hardy Perennial These are frequently used as
bedding, and are able to survive the winter
unprotected. Bergenias and doronicums are
examples suitable for permanent schemes.

F1 Hybrid An F1 hybrid is the result of a con-
trolled cross to achieve exceptional performance and uniformity. F1 seeds are usually
more expensive than open crosses, but they
will reward you with often vastly superior
results. Seed collected from F1 hybrids at
home will not come true.

HALF-HARDY ANNUALS

Mesembryanthemum
(Livingstone Daisy)
Low-growing tender annuals
which need sun and warmth
to produce masses of
daintily rayed flowers in soft
shades of orange, pink and
yellow. The young seedlings
are susceptible to slug
attack but, once matured,
they will perform for long
periods.

Petunia × *hybrida*
A universal bedder in
colours throughout the
spectrum. Technically a
perennial but generally
grown as an annual. New
developments include
trailing kinds, and varieties
that perform well in a damp
summer.

Phlox drummondii
Jewel-like colours on these
tender annuals make them
firm favourites. Most seed
comes in mixtures and
produces blooms in soft
colours but with bright,
contrasting centres.

Tagetes (French and
African Marigolds)
Among the easiest of the
tender annuals, with a
familiar rank aroma – which
is not unpleasant. From
seed, in the right conditions,
many will flower in a few
weeks and keep going all
summer.

NOTE ON VARIETIES

In this book, I have generally avoided giving cultivar names for annuals and half-hardy annuals. This is partly because some varieties are known by different names in catalogues and reference books, but mainly because breeding in these plants is so active and imaginative; so cultivars that are currently popular are likely to be outclassed before long. The joy of bedding is that you only have it for a limited period, so you can experiment happily and

ABOVE *Using lettuce plants as bedding is culinary creativity of an unusual kind.*

cash in on introductions if they tempt you. A lot depends on taste and your own spirit of adventure; it is worth remembering that while novelty may be exciting, it is far wiser to select plants on their record of performance, rather than their outlandish appearance. Reliable varieties of the most popular bedding plants can be found listed in the Plant Directory on page 88.

DESIGN AND THEORY

Planting is an art form, the gardener using plants just as a sculptor works with solid materials or a painter mixes paints. A skilled, creative planter will contrive a series of flowery climaxes to run through the seasons. With permanent mixed planting, this usually takes years to build up, but with bedding, the results can be almost instantaneous. Working with a changing medium requires some skill, not only to maximize the drama at seasonal peaks but also to select plants which can carry the display through quiet periods. Bedding may lack the more subtle nuances of the mixed herbaceous and shrub border but, judiciously planted, will still ensure a long run of lively interest.

LEFT AND ABOVE *Tulips, with their upright nature, bold heads and clean colouring, are the mainstay of most spring bedding displays. They can be underplanted with wallflowers, in complimentary or contrasting colours (left); or with other low growing spring bedding such as double daisies, which will add colour before and after the tulips are in bloom.*

RIGHT *Bedding is often most effective when planted to create precise blocks of colour. These bold groups of dark cannas, red zinnias and salvias, with yellow and orange marigolds, are planted for maximum drama.*

BELOW *If the impact of massed bedding plants can be a little indigestible, a change of texture might lift the scheme. Here the tails of the ornamental grass, Pennisetum villosum, make fluffy companions to late-summer rudbeckias.*

Painting with Bedding

Planting, like painting, is not just about colour. There is so much more to it than merely using the right pigments to create an effect. An artist works to conjure up the desired mood, using sombre colours for dark subjects and light hues for joyful ones. Features on a face might be strongly lit; striped or contrasting blocks of colours create a feeling of unease; soft sweeps of bland colours are restful. Mood is also enhanced by the use of different textures and hues. Even the grain of a picture – the quantity of oil on the canvas, the roughness of the surface – makes a huge difference to the effect.

This analogy fits comfortably in a garden because the painter and the creative planter have, by and large, similar aesthetic objectives. Colour, for example, can be used in solid blocks, in swirling contrasts, in ribbons running along a border edge or as tiny dots on a neutral background. Flowers alone need not supply all the colour in a scheme, for foliage can be used to change the impact: imagine the effect of scarlet pelargoniums interspersed with the silver foliage of *Helichrysum petiolare*. Taken a step further, foliage could play the dominant role within a planting. Think of the contrast of warm and cool colour suggested by planting bronze cannas alongside the glaucous melianthus, or by pairing gold-variegated sage with the purple kind. With foliage combinations as attractive as these, who needs flowers?

Painterly effects in your bedding schemes can be achieved by careful planning, taking account of the fact that with living material, plant textures, different shades of green in the

FORMAL BEDDING
In formal beds, structural design comes from measured planting. Architectural plants act as 'dot' plants, making focal points amidst a sea of massed bedding; such a scheme is often edged with a contrasting border.

INFORMAL BEDDING
Bedding plants for informal schemes are most effective if planted in drifts that weave around the space and intermingle with each other, rather than dotted around indiscriminately. Such a planting plan is more akin to that of a traditional herbaceous border.

leaves, and contrasting colours within each individual flower will all alter the overall effect. Seed mixtures can be particularly difficult to accommodate, since they often blend colours indiscriminately, which can jar.

THE SETTING

Your bedding plants must also fit into their surroundings in the garden. In an informal setting, it is often wise to go for looser, more open planting rather than rigid blocks of colour. In settings where architecture dominates, such as alongside the house or a wall, colour groups might need to be bolder to hold their own, and will certainly need to harmonize. The reds and russets of brickwork often make a better background to cool blues or foliage colours than to oranges or pinks, which might clash. Where walls are painted white, clean bold colours work well, whereas pallid hues could look washed out: crimson fuchsias or bright red roses will work better than pale campanulas or petunias in pastel shades.

In natural plantings, especially between shrubs, the dividing line between 'ground cover' and bedding becomes indistinct. Self-perpetuating ground cover is outside the scope of this book, but where temporary plants are introduced to create particular effects, they can be termed 'bedding', but must blend comfortably into the natural habitat. Dots of strong colours might work but fancy hybrids with big flowers need very careful siting. Spring primroses provide a good example. The wild species is pale yellow and

LEFT *Sweeps of bright red salvias and alonsoa make a strong foreground against tall dahlias and heleniums.*

its early cultivars come in light mauves, brick shades or wine pink. All of these make fine natural-looking bedding displays in carefully placed drifts in the shady border. The modern, florists' primroses, with flowers bred to reach a size of 5cm (2in) and more across, and whose colours include red, orange or scarlet, vivid gold and shocking pink, would, in marked contrast, look garish and forbidding in such a situation.

Nevertheless, because bedding is, for the most part, short term, you can afford to be daring. Having the courage to put the wildest colour combinations or plant compositions to the test might well prove rewarding. If your pluck ends in triumph, you can cheer; but if you loathe the monster you have created, you can derive pleasure from pulling it all up at the end of the season and trying again the following year!

ABOVE *Tubs and hanging baskets make ideal homes for summer bedding. This floriferous display has an unsophisticated charm that is perfect for a traditional narrowboat.*

Informal Bedding

Aspect and conditions: A hot, dry position with plenty of sunshine but thin, rubbly, hungry soil. An old gravel mulch lies on much of the surface.

Scheme: The object was to replant part of a rather run-down terrace with drought-tolerant flowering perennials that would rapidly provide thick growth with plenty of rich colour. A background of shrubs was already *in situ*.

Planting in groups of three or five created bold drifts of colour, and blending the pastel shades of diascia and osteospermum with the more strident hues of pelargoniums and Mexican salvias made for an exciting effect.

Results: The gentle green of the nicotiana flowers and deep chocolate cosmos watered down some of the wilder

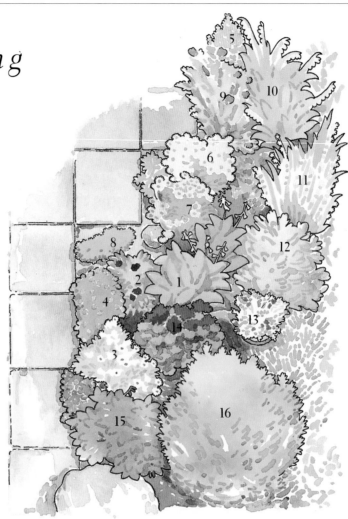

ABOVE *Argyranthemums are some of the easiest and most dependable of the tender perennials. They grow easily from cuttings, and will flower non-stop from late spring until the first heavy frosts.*

colours so that, in spite of such a diversity of shapes, sizes, textures and shades, the whole scheme came together to create a delightful and long-lasting display. The cosmos and salvias did well after rain, while in periods of drought the osteospermums came into their own.

Plants used:

1 *Nicotiana langsdorffii* (seed-raised)
2 *Cosmos atrosanguineus*
3 *Osteospermum* 'Silver Sparkler'
4 *Brachycome iberidifolia*
5 *Diascia* 'Ruby Field'
6 *Argyranthemum* 'Jamaica Primrose'
7 *Argyranthemum* 'Peach Cheeks'
8 *Verbena peruviana*
9 *Glaucium phoenicium*
10 *Digitalis lutea*
11 *Sisyrinchium striatum*
12 *Romneya coulteri*
13 *Pelargonium* 'Summer Showers' with *Helichrysum plecostachys*
14 *Pelargonium* (zonal)
15 *Salvia coccineta*
16 *Daphne burkwoodii*

Sculpting with Bedding

Because it is to do with covering surfaces, we tend to think of bedding as being on one level. This may be the case with some plantings but in a well-designed scheme you can create as much contour as with any other kind of planting. Containers, vertical surfaces and raised beds help to make bedding three dimensional but much of the profile can come from the plants themselves.

A step in the right direction is to select plants that grow to different heights and arrange them with the short ones near the front. Placing plants so that they increase the height of the border in tiers or in a step formation takes profile planning a stage further, and organizing more complicated patterns of height variation takes the technique to its limits. If you then site tall, distinctive 'dot' plants at strategic spots in the bed, you are beginning to approach Victorian sophistication. The classic flower bed would consist of a strong central feature – perhaps a container or a central statue, surrounded by a main area of one, or at the most two, kinds of plant – traditionally such floriferous herbaceous species as pelargoniums, asters or salvias. These massed plants may be divided into compartments with low hedges, or planted in one single block but with different, lower plants marking the boundaries or bringing the level down at the border edge. To break up the whole, a limited series of dot plants would be placed at regular intervals. These would create a contrast in texture and character as well as in stature. Standard fuchsias, spiky plants like cordylines or even young banana trees have all been used in such a way in traditional bedding schemes.

In less formal bedding, too much uniformity would be too rigid, so it is important to make the profile as natural-looking as possible. Planting can still be arranged in bold groups, but works best in the style of a traditional herbaceous border, with seemingly random drifts of each variety appearing to merge with another but never quite mixing. Dot plants are useful here too, but should also be placed randomly so as to look more natural.

Finally, as with all gardening, it pays to think bedding over from a different angle. There is no reason why schemes should be restricted to the horizontal plane. Although furnishing walls and fences is hardly the province of a bedding plant manual, climbing plants themselves certainly are. To achieve height quickly and easily, especially in a small garden, it is a simple task to make temporary supporting structures to be furnished with

fast-growing herbaceous climbers. The structures themselves can be as simple as a bunch of tall bamboo canes, pushed into the ground and tied together at the top to make the shape of a tepee; or a pyramid made from four pieces of fan-shaped trellis, used upside-down (as on page 79); or you can purchase ready-shaped wire or metal frames.

Such plants as *Cobaea scandens*, sweet peas, *Rhodochiton atrosanguineus*, morning glories or the gorgeous *Maurandya erubescens* are all ravishing candidates for adding a vertical dimension to your bedding scheme. Started off under glass and trained tidily, they will flower all summer long.

ABOVE AND LEFT *The role of the dot plant is to anchor the display and give it shape. Above, a dense mass of ageratum is enclosed in a border of* Senecio cineraria, *and interrupted by the statuesque forms of standard fuchsias. Left, the fleshy leaves of* Ensete ventricosum *(banana palm), give a sculptural quality to a bed of low-growing plants.*

A Traditional Scheme

Aspect and conditions: The site has a deep, fertile soil, though rather heavy, in a well-lit position, protected from the west by a tall hornbeam hedge but otherwise open to the winds.

ABOVE Datura inoxia, *with its huge, trumpet flowers and velvety foliage, is a fine example of an architectural dot plant; it needs shelter from wind.*

Scheme: A rectangular plot measuring 3m (10ft) by 2m (7ft) formed the basis for this simplified version of traditional nineteenth-century bedding. As a centrepiece, a small bay tree was clipped in a rounded shape and planted in a terracotta planter. At its base, a contrast was made with young, silver-leaved plants of *Senecio viravira*. At first these were pinched back to promote bushy growth, but later the pale sulphur flowers were allowed to develop.

The main body of the bedding consisted of massed, seed-raised pelargoniums. The F1 strain 'Appleblossom Orbit' made the best choice because, although the leaves are dark with distinctive markings, the flowers are a pale, blush pink. Pure white pansies, planted out in half moon patterns rather than in straight lines at the border's edge, made a bright contrast. Four specimens of *Datura inoxia* sited as dot plants made the finishing touch. When not in flower, their velvety foliage contrasted with the rounded pelargonium leaves; but when they produced their sporadic crops of huge, white, deeply fragrant trumpet flowers, they became focal points.

Results: The period effect was achieved with a very simple scheme using only four kinds of plant plus the bay.

Plants used:
1 *Datura inoxia*
2 *Viola* 'Paper White'
3 *Pelargonium* 'Appleblossom Orbit'
4 *Senecio viravira* (syn. *leucostachys*): from cuttings taken in spring from a stock plant
5 Bay: clipped and grown in a container

GROWING YOUR PLANTS

Bedding uses lots of plants and temporary bedding needs to be replaced each season. Garden centres and other retailers are well placed to supply a huge and hungry market, but it can be less costly and more fun to raise your own. Furthermore, growing from seed and collecting plants from cuttings widens your choice and enables you to develop a growing collection. Often the only limitation is the space you have available for rearing the young plants – in late spring and early summer you can easily find yourself overrun. Included in this chapter are some tips to help you spread the work, and a year planner to indicate when you need to get your plans under way.

LEFT *With minimal facilities and only modest skill, colourful plants like nemesias, petunias – this one is called 'Plum Pudding' – and the vivid gaillardias are easy to raise.*

ABOVE *Dahlias can be lifted at the end of summer and overwintered. They can be replanted the following year, and used as a source of cuttings for future seasons.*

Succeeding with Seed

The cheapest way of producing your own plants is to grow them from seed. Anyone can manage the easiest – hardy annuals – simply by scattering the seed on the soil and waiting for it to spring to life, flowering in no more than a few weeks. Most hardy perennials are almost as easy but take longer to germinate. Tender plants – and a heavy proportion of bedding is tender – need a little more care, but even with these, the growing techniques are far less complicated than they sometimes appear.

Having the right equipment helps. If you plan to do much in the way of planting each year, a greenhouse will transform the process from 'making do' on crowded windowsills to going into proper plant production. For raising tender plants, your greenhouse will need to be heated to keep it free of frost, and, if you can run to a heated propagator as well, your seed-raising problems will be significantly reduced.

If a greenhouse is out of the question, windowsill propagation is a realistic alternative and, in careful hands, can work well, although there will be a limit on the range of plants you will be able to produce. Several manufacturers make effective windowsill propagation equipment, but windowsill-raised plants will tend to be more leggy and less robust than greenhouse-raised ones simply because of the lower light levels.

You will also need a cold frame for acclimatizing young plants before bedding them out. This can be a simple and makeshift affair made from a couple of wooden boxes with panes of glass or plastic laid on top, or you can build one quite cheaply from brick or timber. Purpose-built frames are widely available in easily assembled kit form.

PLANNING

The most common mistake enthusiastic beginners make when raising their own seed is to underestimate the phenomenon of growth. Take a packet of pelargonium seeds, for instance. If the seed is good quality and your management is up to scratch, twenty seeds will produce at least 18 seedlings. These will fit easily into a quarter-size seed tray. Pricked out into twenty 8cm (3in) pots, their space requirements expand dramatically. Yet these pots will accommodate them for only about a month, after which they'll need potting up into 13cm (5in) pots. At first these can touch, but

LEFT A *single seed packet can produce a crop of mesembryanthemums this large for no more than the cost of the seed, a little greenhouse heat, and your own labour.*

before the plants are ready to be planted out they will be big enough to need spacing further apart. Thus, from the original 20 × 10cm (8 × 4in) tray, you could end up needing nearly 2.5 square metres, or 8 square feet, of greenhouse staging! And you cannot put anything outside because there is still risk of a fatal frost.

The solution to this is to work out roughly how much space you can spare and then decide which seeds will receive priority, and how to stagger their production. In mild areas, you can relieve pressure on space by stocking your cold frame up to a month or at the most six weeks before the date when the last frosts might be expected. You will need to be vigilant, though, and be prepared to give the plants extra protection by securing blanketing material such as gardener's polypropylene fleece on top of the plants at night during cold snaps.

Most seed packets will produce far more seedlings than you need, so to relieve pressure on the greenhouse or cold frame, be prepared to discard a proportion, only pricking out as many seedlings as you need into pots or pans. Keep the unpricked-out seedlings in reserve in case of accidents or disasters with the young plants.

RIGHT *Pansies are among the easiest of bedding plants to raise from seed as they are fully hardy, so need no artificial heat for rearing.*

SOWING SEED

Wash and sterilize a seed tray. Half-fill it with sterile compost, and water it using a rose on the watering can. Leave it for a few hours to drain, then sow average-sized seed evenly on the surface.

With very light seed, such as lobelia, it can be hard to see how densely you have sprinkled it. Mix a little silver sand into the seed packet, then 'sow' this. Cover the tray with a thin layer of sand.

Large seeds, such as those of calendula or nasturtium, can be sown individually into plug trays. Fill the trays only lightly with compost, as compressing it can make the plants difficult to get out.

GERMINATING THE SEED

All seeds vary in their germination requirements. Some need frost to crack their coats before they can imbibe water and begin the life process; some need darkness, some light; some require warmth. The first task therefore, even for the experienced gardener, is to read the directions on the packet.

Most seeds are successful if sown on to the surface of damp compost and covered with a thin layer of more compost or horticultural sand. Perlite can be used too, although I find it becomes unmanageable when it dries out: it blows away easily, and is difficult to re-wet. The covering needs to be relatively light, however, so that the seedlings can push through easily, so the compost or sand should be sieved over the sown seed.

Most tender bedding plants germinate readily in compost at between 15°C and 25°C (60-77°F) – easily achieved on a sunny windowsill in the house, in a greenhouse, or using a heated propagator. Germination times vary according to variety but if nothing happens within a couple of weeks, do not give up hope – particularly when sowing batches of different species. Some will appear almost overnight, others may take as long as a month to emerge.

SOME BASIC RULES

It is impossible to generalize for all seed-sowing techniques because of the different requirements for different plants, but the following rules should be followed, no matter what.

Hygiene The fungal disease known as 'damping off' ruins more seed crops and dashes more hopes than anything else. Always use *clean* seed trays or pots, fresh, *sterile* compost, and water it only with pure water from the tap, not rainwater from the water butt.

Compost Special seed-sowing compost with low nutrients works best. I use peat- or organic-based products from reputable manufacturers. Some 'peat alternatives' work well, others are too fibrous and prone to saturation. Compost must always be moist but never saturated. Water thoroughly some hours *before* sowing, rather than after.

Firm gently Seed must be in tight contact with the compost so that it can absorb moisture, but the compost should not be compacted so that all the air has been squashed out of it. This will merely rot the seeds.

PREPARING FOR GERMINATION

Suitable coverings for sown seed include sieved compost, fine sand, sphagnum moss peat, or perlite (illustrated). The covering should be lightweight, and both water absorbent and freely draining.

Cover the seed trays with milky polythene to maintain warmth and humidity. Check every day for signs of the first seed leaves. As soon as these appear, remove the polythene and move the trays into full light.

Alternatively, place the trays inside a propagator in full light, and cover. For most seeds, maintain the heat at around 21°C/70°F. Water germinated seeds lightly if the compost becomes dry.

Do not disturb The surface of the seed tray should be left undisturbed until such time as the seedlings pop up. This means watering from below – if watering is necessary – and taking care not to disturb the compost.

Sow thinly The seed should be scattered on the compost so that there is a big enough gap between seeds to allow each seedling to develop without competition from its neighbour. Experience helps here but, as a general rule, sow too thinly, never too thickly. Trays that have been sown thickly need extra care when pricking out.

Prick out early As soon as the emerged seedlings are large enough to handle, remove the trays from the propagator, place them in an airy, warm environment, and prick them out as soon as you possibly can.

Be relaxed This may appear to be a silly rule but it is so easy to kill your babies with kindness. Once sown, keep an eye on the trays but try to resist the temptation to keep touching or looking at them. Disturbance reduces your chances of success.

PRICKING OUT

Pricking out is easy once you have got over the awkwardness of handling tiny plantlets. My method is to tease individual seedlings from the seedling compost with a sharp stick, then, holding the seedling very gently by one leaf, I lower the roots into the hole I have already dibbed for them in the new compost. Depending on the size of the plants, you can prick out either into trays, individual pots or into plug trays.

PRICKING OUT

As soon as the seedlings are large enough to handle, they can be pricked out and replanted into clean trays or pots. These pansies are going into 7cm (3in) pots, where they can stay until planting out.

Plants from Cuttings

Much of our heritage of garden plants can be reproduced vegetatively and the almost universal method which suits every gardener, from raw beginner to practised expert, is to take cuttings.

Named cultivars of such plants as fuchsias, pelargoniums, verbenas and perennial wallflowers will only reproduce vegetatively since they cannot breed true from seed. Others, such as salvia species and penstemons, root so quickly and easily that cuttings are the best method. Many of these species can be over-wintered under glass as mature stock plants, and used as a source of cutting material in autumn or spring.

As with seed, a propagator makes things easier but, unlike seedlings,

young cuttings cope far better with low light levels. Direct sunlight can burn up the tissue before the cutting has had a chance to develop roots.

The method varies according to the kind of plant and to the time of year. Woody plants can be propagated either from softwood cuttings, taken in the growing season, or from ripened slips or twigs, taken at any time during the dormant period. Most bedding is raised from softwood cuttings so our notes here will dwell on that method.

You can take cuttings at any time, but the optimum season is midsummer, after the longest day but before the nights have begun to cool. Select young vigorous shoots and gather them into a plastic bag to keep them turgid.

Fill trays, pots or pans with a gritty free-draining compost and firm it down; most cuttings will fit comfortably into 9cm (3½in) pots for the first few weeks. Trim the lower leaves off each cutting, as any leaf left in contact with the compost is likely to cause rotting, and cut it across at or just below a leaf joint. If you want to you can dip the end of the cutting in rooting powder or gel. Dib a hole in the compost with a pencil or sharp object, and set the cutting in so that its

LEFT AND OPPOSITE TOP *Many tender perennials are easy to raise from cuttings taken in summer and overwintered under protection. Penstemons (left), verbenas and iresine (opposite top) are examples.*

base is in contact with the bottom of the hole. Firm the cutting in. Place the trays or pots in a lightly shaded propagator, or place a plastic bag upside-down over the pot, sealing it full of air, to create a humid atmosphere.

Most plants will produce a shock of roots within a few weeks. Once the cutting is firm within its compost, indicating that roots have formed, you will need to pot it up into the next size of pot, using fresh potting compost.

Newly rooted cuttings will form neat, uniform plants but some species benefit from having their main shoots pinched out to encourage production of side shoots. Pelargoniums sometimes grow lanky with naked stems, but this is easily cured by cutting off the top to stimulate side-shoots. The top can be rooted as an extra cutting!

Certain plants, particularly dendranthemas (chrysanthemums) and dahlias, perform well when grown from basal cuttings; basal cuttings are actually the shoots that the plant naturally throws up from its base. Taking the cuttings is a late winter or early spring activity and requires a little more preparation than simply snapping off a shoot or two from the growing plant. Mature roots sometimes called 'stools' are planted up, in winter, in deep trays in the greenhouse. Within a short time, stout young shoots emerge from the old roots. These are removed with the aid of a sharp knife, and can be potted up and rooted in a warm greenhouse. A young plant with a single stem soon forms, and once the danger of frost is passed, it can be planted outdoors as part of a scheme.

Certain speedy bedding plants can be multiplied rapidly from cuttings during the second half of winter. No harm will come by taking cuttings of cuttings of cuttings, bulking up your numbers until a single plant has yielded literally hundreds of progeny. Verbenas will allow this treatment, as will certain lobelias. The old trailing kind, *Lobelia erinus*, will root as it runs and can be bulked up surprisingly fast, especially during short days when it tends to produce vegetative shoots rather than flowering ones.

TAKING CUTTINGS

Select clean, vigorous, non-flowering shoots. Remove the lower leaves and re-cut the stems across a leaf node. Dib holes in the compost in pots or trays, place the cutting in and firm the compost.

Rooting is accelerated if cuttings are placed in a propagator with bottom heat of 21-25°C/70-77°F. Shade from direct sunlight and ventilate on hot days. Once new growth appears, pot each cutting on.

OVERWINTERING STOCK PLANTS

Dendranthemas and dahlias should be lifted in autumn, cut back to 25cm/10in, and planted in trays for overwintering. In late winter, strong shoots from their bases can be removed and rooted.

Achieving Healthy Plants

One advantage of raising your own plants is that you have more control over their management. If your management is good, your plants will be. The objective, for successful bedding, is to make sure that the plants are growing steadily right up to the point where they are planted out – and then to continue for the whole season.

Time operations accurately Some species need sowing months before bedding out. I like to sow pelargonium seeds around the shortest day, for instance, but will not plant them outdoors until five months later. Quick annuals like marigolds or cornflowers, on the other hand, may flower less than ten weeks after sowing.

Feed the plants regularly Feeding on a regular basis, and giving the plants adequate space under cover, will help to ensure good specimens. Manufactured compost contains plantfood which will last for several weeks before you need to begin feeding; thereafter feed weekly or fortnightly, depending on how fast the plants are growing. Watch for signs of plant 'hunger' – paling of the leaves, less vigorous growth – and feed as soon as these signs appear.

Re-pot whenever necessary Never put small plants into too large a pot, as this can cause rotting, but re-pot as soon as roots begin to emerge through the drainage holes. Re-pot in stages so that the new container is never more than 3cm (1in) bigger than the previous one.

Sometimes, if the planting out time approaches and the plants are getting nearly potbound, you will need to decide whether to plant out a little early – and risk a damaging late frost – or to re-pot for their last couple of weeks.

Provide plenty of light The biggest limiting factor, where plant raising is concerned, is likely to be the availability of sunlight. Where plants are raised on windowsills – even well-lit ones – they are likely to be drawn towards the light and grow leggy. This can happen even in a well-sited greenhouse, particularly during winter when days are short, or when the plants are overcrowded and competing for light. Therefore only grow what you can accommodate and limit windowsill production to as short a period as possible.

Deal with problems promptly Move leggy plants into the light quickly and

Well grown plants will always provide the best flowers for the longest period. For these sweet williams, plenty of feed and water has ensured a stunning display.

pinch out their main shoots to promote bushiness. Watch for signs of damping off and, where this occurs, prick out surviving seedlings with great care and discard all affected compost.

HARDENING OFF

Tender bedding plants raised from cuttings or seed sown in late winter and early spring will be ready for planting outdoors as soon as the weather is 'safe' and as soon as they have been 'hardened off' – that is, fully acclimatized to outdoor conditions. This is best carried out in a cold frame. At first, cover the plants at night with the glass lid. Later, leave the lid ajar, and gradually increase their exposure to the outside temperature as the weeks progress. Three weeks is the optimum period for hardening off.

When can you plant out, and therefore start the hardening-off process? The so-called frost-free date is a notional event. In most years, the last frost of the season occurs several weeks before the accepted date for the last *possible* frost in your area, but it can freeze right up to the date and occasionally even beyond it! The imprudent gardener might be tempted to plant out early but this is foolhardy, even when the weather looks set to be balmy and gentle. In the event of late frost, there is little that can be done, although plants that have been properly hardened off are more likely to survive the setback.

Buying your Bedding

Absorbing fun though propagating is, not everyone has the time or the inclination for it. The alternative is to buy your bedding in, and this is a perfectly viable option – indeed, it is the choice of the majority of gardeners. Happily, almost everyone with a garden is likely to buy a few colourful plants each summer, and the market is therefore geared to a huge sale of bedding every spring. Less discriminating planters have an unhealthy predilection for colour mixtures rather than single shades, which can limit the field somewhat for colour-conscious buyers; but there is usually a good range of self-coloured bedding stock available.

It helps to know exactly what you want. Translated into bedding, this may not amount to a detailed knowledge of specific varieties available, but rather to having a clear idea of the shapes, sizes, colours and habits of the plants. If, for instance, you want to plant a red theme with a graduated profile that will give height and plenty of colour late in the autumn as well as in early summer, you can then find out what plants on sale will meet your needs. Be prepared to be flexible in your choice of plants but hold fast to your design.

Garden centres can be a glorious and bewildering mass of enticingly coloured bedding plants in spring. Plant breeders have tended to select varieties which look colourful at point of sale – but which may have poorer lasting qualities than older varieties which, though they may be slower to come into flower, sustain their displays throughout the season. Do not be seduced, therefore, by flowers alone but rather be guided by the reliability of the variety.

While you are at the plant centre, it makes sense to look over all the plants on sale, rather than just the bedding. A large number of perennials and several shrubs could be incorporated into your bedding theme and then moved to perform a different function after the bedding has been stripped out. Imagine the gloss on the leaves of a camellia: what a perfect dot plant that could make for your bedding scheme, but what a useful spring shrub for next year into the bargain!

A number of nurseries now offer baby plants ready grown in tiny plugs. This is an excellent way of raising young plants if you lack a greenhouse or feel unable to meet the challenge of growing from seed. If you purchase very young plants by mail order, be sure to unwrap them the very moment they arrive and plant them up within the day.

QUALITY CONTROL

Once you have made up your mind which plants to buy, you will need to check them for quality. Bedding plants at point of sale should be healthy, growing with vigour, but not yet pot-bound. Size does not really matter, as long as smaller size is reflected proportionately in a lower price, but you need to remember that small plants will take longer to begin their display.

Watch for signs of neglect or poor aftercare. Dry compost is obvious. Plants that have been starved of water and then soaked are harder to spot, but will often display uneven development in the trays. Plants that have been chilled will show darkened foliage. Beware, too, of over-soft plants, still lush from the glasshouse and inadequately hardened off.

Price is important but not the overriding factor. The real savings are to be made by selecting the very best plants – the finest varieties and the best-raised plants. After all, the whole point of bedding is to create a really good display and if you do not use good plants, you are handicapped from the start.

Look for healthy foliage and well developed roots (these are ageratums).

Planning, Planting and Aftercare

Bedding is hungry. Plants that are expected to grow from seed to, in some cases, a metre or more in a single season will need plenty of fertilizer, and good, rich, well tended soil. Like people, they will always perform best in a climate free of stress and full of sunshine.

PREPARING THE SITE

Good soil preparation is essential for best results; indeed, it is more important with bedding than with most other forms of ornamental gardening. Ensure that the bed is free of weeds, particularly the perennial kinds. Build up organic matter in the soil by incorporating plenty of well-made garden compost or, if you are lucky enough to find a source, well rotted farmyard manure; failing these commodities, any rottable organic matter will help.

About a week before planting, rake in a general compound fertilizer rich in nitrogen, phosphorus and potassium, at the manufacturers' recommended rates.

PLANNING AND PLANTING

Complex, formal bedding schemes need to be measured out and marked out on the ground, before you plant the young plants. Some people use silver sand to do this, but I find string tied to short canes is a better, more flexible method of dividing up a large space into the shapes I want. However you do it, place all the plants out in their intended positions *before* planting, so that final adjustments to design and plant spacing can be made before you are committed.

In theory, plants should be set out at the spacing recommended on the seed packet. In practice, you can plant a little denser; although if you crowd them, the plants will be in greater competition for nutrients, water and light, so may not develop properly.

Water plants in thoroughly and water again several times until they are well established and clearly growing well. I like to water new transplants with a very weak solution of liquid feed – about a quarter the recommended strength.

SETTING OUT A SCHEME

Planting schemes begin with careful measurement. Prepare your soil and site carefully, then mark out your scheme on the ground with canes and string. Establish the centre by crossing diagonal strings across the plot, and use this as an anchor point. Position your key plants first.

With the anchor plants in position, it makes sense to play safe and set out the plants for the rest of the bed in their pots, before the actual planting process begins: you may want to make a few changes, and if the number of plants you have is limited, you can space them more effectively.

SIMPLE SCHEMES

If the bedding scheme is relatively simple, and you have plenty of plants available, a bedding pattern can be marked out with plants themselves. Establish lines of plants first to divide the area into manageable shapes, as shown in this circular bed, then fill in the spaces.

SPACING THE PLANTS

Seed packets give full information about the spacing for the plants. Initially, spacing out the plants as directed can give the bed a rather contrived look (above), but once they have grown and merged, the scheme will look natural and the even spacing will ensure no gaps (below).

AFTERCARE

Compared to the work involved in rearing young plants, the aftercare of a bedding scheme is not especially onerous. These are the basic points to remember.

Water regularly This is the most important job, especially in dry spells.

Feed once If the soil was well prepared, the plants will need no more than one liquid feed later in the season.

Weed the beds Pull out any weeds as soon as they appear, especially when the bedding is newly planted – the weeds will only crowd out your precious plants.

Watch for pests and diseases This is especially important in the early stages, when slugs and snails in particular will be tempted by the young shoots.

Dead-head assiduously Regular dead-heading ensures a long-lasting display.

PESTS AND DISEASES

Pests and diseases should not pose problems to well grown bedding. Plant breeders are constantly producing new, disease-resistant varieties and it is always worth looking out for these as they become available.

At the rearing stages, aphids and red spider mite can be troublesome and thrips can damage flowers to a considerable extent, especially in hot, sultry weather conditions. Control by spraying.

Vine weevils can devastate fuchsias and some other plants. They are controllable by biological methods.

Newly planted bedding can suffer attacks by slugs and snails. There are products that can be used against them, but some are less environmentally friendly than others. In small bedding schemes, mechanical deterrents, such as sharp grit laid around susceptible plants, can be effective.

Mildew can attack vulnerable plants such as asters; spraying can control it.

The remedy for most of these pests and diseases outdoors is to provide the best possible growing conditions and allow the plants' natural vigour to carry them through. Most summer bedding, therefore, makes fine material for the all-organic gardener!

STRIPPING OUT

Autumn will be the major time for stripping out. Most of the summer's bedding will be destined for the compost heap, but perennial plants and shrubs, such as fuchsias, can be used year after year. If they are tender they need winter protection, and must therefore be potted up or planted in the greenhouse, where the shorter days will slow down their growth rate. During this period, and again when growth begins in spring, cuttings can be taken to provide new plant material; in many cases the old plants will also be reusable in the next year's scheme.

Bedding schemes for the spring can be planted after the autumn clearance, and any problems such as outbreaks of perennial weeds or soil damage put right. With bare soil in front of you, and a fertile imagination, now is the time to begin dreaming up even bigger and better ideas for next year!

MANAGING BULBS

Most of this chapter has dealt with the raising of summer plants, but summer is only one of four seasons. Spring displays can be just as spectacular and the biggest contribution here comes from flowering bulbs.

Autumn is planting time for spring bulbs and can coincide with the stripping out of summer bedding. It is important to plant bulbs as fresh as possible so, if you have to store them for a while after buying them, keep them cool but never frosted, and neither too damp nor dried out. Clearly, the safest place for a bulb to rest is in the ground!

Bulbs should be planted deeply. Tulips do well if they are planted as deeply as 15 to 20cm (6-8in) and, at those depths, can be left in situ and planted over with subsequent bedding schemes. They may not multiply, and the flowers tend to get smaller over a period of time, but you will find that they will give several seasons of trouble-free service. Feeding is beneficial at and after flowering time, but in practice most bulbs seem to soldier on even when totally neglected.

Although the foliage of dying bulbs can be unsightly, it is soon masked by the emerging foliage of other plants. But if tulips or other bulbs get in the way, you can lift the bulbs after flowering and partially replant them elsewhere in the garden while the leaves die down.

Summer bulbs play a useful role in bedding schemes. Galtonia, gladiolus and the garlic tribe have several species perfect for bedding. Many also seed freely, which can be an advantage in species that reach flowering size within a couple of seasons. Bulbs of tender species such as gladiolus must be lifted in autumn, allowed to dry off, and over-wintered in pans of barely damp compost, set in a frost-free place.

While shrubs creep slowly into leaf in spring, tulips develop at an astonishing rate to provide bold, colourful displays.

A Bedding Planner

SIX WEEKS AFTER SHORTEST DAY

Greenhouse
- Sow slow-developing bedding plants such as zonal pelargoniums directly into plugs or into seed pans.
- Sow early, hardy bedding such as antirrhinums.

Outdoors
- Dead-head winter-flowering pansies.
- Make sure wallflowers are not being rocked by the wind.

MIDWINTER TO MID-SPRING

Greenhouse or windowsill propagation
- Sow the main run of half-hardy annuals in plugs or seed pans.
- Prick out early sown bedding into seed trays – with pelargoniums, for example, 40 plants to the tray.
- Start overwintered tender perennials into gentle growth by removing old top-growth, watering and gentle feeding.
- Take basal cuttings of derdranthemas and dahlias.

Outdoors
Apply manures or mulches to beds not occupied with spring bedding.

MID TO LATE SPRING

Greenhouse or windowsill
- Sow quicker annuals such as French or African marigolds.
- Sow hardy annuals such as cornflowers or lavatera.

- Pot up early sown bedding.
- Take basal cuttings of tender perennials such as argyranthemums, perennial salvias and penstemons. Strike these with bottom heat in a gritty compost and pot up as soon as they are rooted.

Outdoors
- Direct sow hardy annuals.
- Plant summer bulbs such as gladiolus.
- Strip out exhausted spring bedding as it comes to the end of its life. Then prepare the ground for summer bedding by digging, and feeding by dressing with manure or artificial fertilizer plus compost. Spring bulbs such as tulips can be carefully lifted and replanted elsewhere to die down, before they are collected up, dried off and stored for replanting next year.
- Plan your planting according to what you have raised.

LATE SPRING TO MIDSUMMER

Greenhouse
- Clear out the last of the bedding and clean up.
- Strike cuttings of perennial wall-flowers and any extra tender perennials.

Outdoors
- Delay planting out until risk of frost is minimal.
- Harden off bedding plants over at least two weeks before final planting. Have protective polypropylene fleece available in case frost is forecast.
- Prepare and plant up containers.

MIDSUMMER UNTIL MID-AUTUMN

Outdoors
- Enjoy your summer bedding! Pick over your displays regularly, dead-head assiduously and keep any weeds at bay.
- Sow seeds of such winter and spring bedding as forget-me-nots, winter pansies and wallflowers.
- Take cuttings of pinks, most shrubs, herbaceous perennials and tender perennials.

MID-AUTUMN TO SHORTEST DAY

Greenhouse
- Begin to build up a collection of tender perennials, either lifted from outside or, preferably, from summer-taken cuttings. (Many of these will make pretty greenhouse plants through the early part of winter).
- Plan your bedding for next summer.
- Accommodate valuable containerized shrubs such as bay trees.

Outdoors
- Sow sweet peas.
- Plant spring bulbs.
- Strip out summer bedding and plant winter and spring displays. Do not over-feed the ground but ensure that spring bedding goes into clean, moist – but not saturated – friable soil.

USING COLOUR

Nothing excites the emotions so strongly as colour. The hues on the spectrum are all important in themselves, but how they are used in conjunction with each other needs very careful consideration. In the realm of garden-ing, the discussion can never limit itself to abstract theory, because plants are such endlessly changing organisms – and in any case, there is almost always a background of green foliage and stems, which neutralizes flower colours and is an additional consideration when predicting the

outcome of a colour combination. Where planting is naturalistic, flower colour, though still import-ant, plays a quieter role than in traditional bed-ding schemes where flowers are massed for drama.

LEFT AND ABOVE *The boldest statements come from using complementary colours. Blue against yellow is especially striking here (left), with the rudbeckias and* Salvia 'Victoria'. *The dahlias 'Geerling's Elite' (above) have a highly effective colour scheme all of their own.*

USING THE COLOUR WHEEL

Colour contrasts

Flower harmonies

One-colour schemes

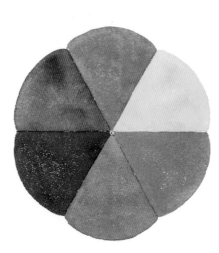

On the colour wheel, the three primary colours, red, yellow and blue, are separated from each other by the secondary colours which they make when mixed: so red and yellow are separated by orange. Neighbouring colours harmonize, colours opposite each other contrast. In the garden, the basic rules can be interpreted in many ways. Green almost always provides the background colour, and white can be used to separate strong colour pairings, or as a highlight for a scheme.

Colour Theory

White light consists of radiant energy whizzing through space. As Isaac Newton discovered, light beams are split into their component rays when they pass through a prism (or a raindrop) and result in the familiar spectrum of red, orange, yellow, green, blue, indigo and violet.

The colours we encounter every day are made up from impure mixes of these pure spectral tones and appear as they do because of three essential characteristics: hue, saturation and tone. Hue is the name of the colour – blue, for instance – and saturation is the quantity of hue in the colour. Thus, a gentian is blue in hue and high in saturation. Flax is also blue, but at lower saturation. Tone represents the light value of the colour. Thus, for example, the deep blue sea has a lower tone than a bright blue sky.

THE COLOUR WHEEL

Flower gardeners need to be familiar with the workings of the colour wheel because an understanding of how colour theory works can dramatically improve the colour quality of a scheme. The colour wheel consists of a disc divided into segments, each of which is a pure colour. The wheel shows how the hues are related to each other: opposing each other (and opposite each other on the wheel) are the three primary colours blue, yellow and red. All other colours result from mixtures of these and their segments are positioned between the primary colours that make them up.

Technically, opposite colours accentuate each other. That is to say, if blue and red are used side by side, the blue looks bluer and the red looks redder. Enhancing colour intensity in this way can be a useful trick. Having said that, however, abstract colour theory has limited value in the garden, because flowers always appear against the backdrop of at least their own foliage. The green has the effect of separating the colours and diluting the drama of a scheme that might have looked bright or loud on paper.

THE EFFECTS OF COLOURS

Colour stimulates different emotions in the onlooker. Blues, lemons and greens are cool and soothing; oranges and reds are fiery and exciting. Most colours have also become associated with a specific meaning: red equals blood equals danger, for instance, but red plus green equals Christmas and all those seasonal good feelings.

Colours interact with each other and with their surroundings. Dots of bright orange or red against a dark background look bigger than they really are, an effect that is important for siting conspicuous flowers. Pale colours light up in the evening, when hot reds tend to disappear. Hard contrasts between warm and cool colours can be dramatic – cornflower blue against mustard yellow, for example – but more closely associated colours harmonize, the one complementing the other.

OPPOSITE TOP AND RIGHT *Two highly dramatic approaches to colour harmonies. Opposite, asters from a seed mixture make a pastel scheme; right, purples, mauves and blues are planted in blocks among silver foliage, with white to lighten the effect.*

REDS

Alonsoa warscewiczii
An endless succession of bright red flowers, borne on darker red stems, makes this a happy bedder for a red scheme. Technically a perennial, but easiest to raise each year from seed.

Dahlia coccinea
A delightful pure species with vivid scarlet flowers, but also dainty enough to make a refreshing change from the more strident blooms of the hybrid dahlias. Easily grown from tubers, which need lifting and storing indoors in winter.

Salvia blepharophylla
A low-growing perennial with a creeping rootstock and shiny foliage. A succession of brilliant red flowers is produced during the second half of the growing season. Prefers moist soil but full sun.

Verbena peruviana
Smaller and neater than most bedding forms of verbena, and often grown as an alpine. Low mats of roughened, lobed foliage are smothered in late summer with glowing scarlet blooms. Not hardy, but easy to propagate by division.

Strong and Hot Colours

In any situation, red, orange and strident yellow make the loudest statements. Bright, sunlit conditions bring out the best in them: whereas brilliant colours can look garish in dull weather, they tone down in strong sunshine. At its simplest, a hot scheme could consist of brilliant red – salvias, say, or pelargoniums – contrasted with hard yellow calceolarias or African marigolds. The effect is restless and jazzy, but in dreary surroundings, what a dramatic flourish!

The boldest of hot schemes are perhaps more appropriate to public places such as traffic islands, where maximum floral impact is needed. In the domestic garden, a gentler combination is usually desirable: bedding can work well when it consists of solid blocks of colour, but the results are generally more satisfying when a scheme does not stray too far from nature, where the background colour is usually green. That means composing the scheme with plenty of foliage to temper some of the hardest colours.

To return to the 'loud' plants mentioned above, African marigolds and red pelargoniums could be made gentler if they were set among the foliage of bronze fennel, dark-leaved coleus or coppery amaranthus, together with plenty of greenery. Use either the red or the orange flower on its own, and the aesthetic qualities of the bedding scheme will improve even further. For example, the red could be blended with silver foliage for a leavening effect, or set around a dark-leaved shrub for a more sombre group.

Warm colours often have softer permutations, and here the line between hot and cool colours blurs. Bronze foliage varies widely and can be warm without shouting: heliotrope, for example, has bronze to purple leaves which can make it useful for toning down a hot scheme – although it might be too strident for a cool one. Flowers, too, can be gentle in their coloration even if their basic hues are anything but cool. Those in the salmon to apricot range, as well as browns, beiges, buffs and russets, although they might be less obvious than the clean colours of the spectrum, are of great value. *Verbena* 'Peaches and Cream' is a soft brick tone, there are nicotianas in 'antique' shades, and the tulip variety 'Apricot Beauty' fades almost to beige. Blending such colours with 'moody' foliage can produce original and charming results; although they will not be good partners to the traditional 'hot' colours of orange, red and strong yellow.

OPPOSITE *The fiery glow of* Salvia splendens *has wrecked many a tasteful bedding scheme. Far better to use it with other bright colours, such as velvety sweet williams and brash dahlias – then the effect is truly dazzling.*

BELOW *In full sun and well-drained soil*, Eschscholzia californica (*California poppies*) *make a welcome splash. They are hardy annuals, and easy to grow from seed sprinkled in the planting position in autumn or spring.*

PLANT PARTNERS

It is perfectly possible to plant hot colours to contrast with cool ones. Red and blue work very well together, either when the blue is pure – without any pink or mauve in it – or when plants are included to make a harmonious transition from red through to crimson, purple, mauve and finally blue. But even these rules are not hard and fast: red penstemons such as 'Garnet' associate well with the lavender-blue of ageratum or with lavender itself – a splendid bedding plant for all sorts of situations. I have seen bright red bedding roses planted with an edging of the dark, purple-blue *Lavandula* 'Hidcote' to create not only a fine piece of bedding, but one that will endure for many years.

Planting partners need not come from the ranks of other bedding plants. For a 'hot' spring scheme in the ochreous colour ranges, yellow tulips, doronicums and bronze winter-

FAR LEFT *This relaxed, uninhibited planting features brightly coloured annuals. In strong sunlight, a rule-breaking combination of red, pink and orange works well.*

LEFT *Height, vivid colours and soft, feathery foliage all make* Cosmos *a fine bedding subject. Here it makes a background for hot-coloured zinnias.*

ABOVE *Dousing hot colours with cool: standard roses in a brash orange provide bursts of strong colour above a misty sea of cool blue lavender. Such contrasts give dramatic 'bite' to a garden.*

flowering pansies could set off the forests of crimson-red shoots of pollarded dogwood, such as *Cornus alba* 'Aurea'. Later, this shrub obliges with golden foliage that could provide the backing for black-and-orange rudbeckias.

For durability, dahlias are superb value, many coming in glowing colours and flowering irrepressibly until the first real frost blackens them. Most have unremarkable leaves but one, 'Bishop of Llandaff', has deeply burnished, almost black foliage.

DIFFICULT SITES

Creating warm-looking displays is more difficult in shade. In dappled shade with moist soil, mimulus – the monkey flower – provides a warmth of colour more usually found among flowers for open, sunny borders. Impatiens, too, dislike sun and have excellent red forms which blend with more permanent plants. And invasive though they are, Welsh poppies (*Meconopsis cambrica*) form drifts of radiant acid yellow or warm tangerine. There are single and double flowered forms, all of which seed freely in shade and moist soil.

ABOVE LEFT *Wallflowers are popular spring bedding. Their colours can be fiery, ranging from yellow to rusts and bronzes.*

LEFT *Strong hot colour can be developed with foliage as well as with flower. Here, the orange and yellow zinnia variety 'Golden Sun' contrasts with the rich purple-bronze leaf of* Ricinus communis *'Impala'.*

OPPOSITE *Warm, glowing colours reach a climax at summer's end with such plants as rudbeckias, most varieties of which flower well into autumn.*

ORANGES AND YELLOWS

Coreopsis
Daisy flowers that come in glowing tones from acid yellow to a rusty tan. Many are perennials, but need to be divided and replanted at least every other year.

Gaillardia
Bi-coloured red and yellow flowers give the effect of orange when grown in a mass. Gaillardia is technically a perennial, but is short-lived, and easy to raise from seed. It is almost constantly in flower.

Tithonia rotundifolia
Rich, glowing orange blooms, reminiscent of dahlias but unique in their colour. Easily raised from seed, the Mexican sunflowers will create a burning accent in even the hottest of bedding schemes.

Zinnia
A range of plants in the daisy family which are almost as good for cutting as for bedding. Shapes and sizes vary from small pompons to large, semi-open blooms, but most of the colours are in the warm range of orange, red and yellow. There are also pinks, mauves and lime green.

Red and Bronze

Aspect and conditions: A partially shaded site with morning sun but in shadow for much of the day. The soil is heavy and damp and inclined to crack in periods of drought.

ABOVE Salvia gesneriiflora, *with its curiously furry red flowers, makes a good contrast to the purple cotinus foliage.*

Scheme: A plot 2.5m (9ft) by 2m (7ft) had a large, pollarded, purple smoke bush positioned slightly off-centre. The bush produced a thick mass of deep purple foliage, forming a dramatic focal point for a scheme of red flowers and coloured leaves. The bedding was planted in naturalistic drifts, rather than in carefully measured blocks, to achieve a relaxed effect. Silver foliage from the senecio was a highlight during dull weather and at dusk, but in sunlight the vibrancy of the red flowers gave the display its strength.

Results: The red hues of the two species of salvia and three different varieties of pelargonium all appeared to clash, but this did not jar the senses, even on close inspection. Slugs caused problems, especially with the coleus, which did not in any case take kindly to the cold, heavy soil; but a lucky germination of self-sown bronze fennel delivered an unexpected but welcome bonus. Its feathery foliage proved to be the perfect foil for the brooding colours and larger leaves of the coleus and pelargoniums.

Plants used:

1 *Cotinus coggygria* 'Royal Purple': a mature shrub already *in situ*, but pollarded for the scheme
2 *Senecio* 'Silver Dust'
3 *Salvia gesneriiflora*
4 *Salvia blepharophylla*
5 Seedlings of bronze fennel, self-sown by lucky chance
6 *Coleus* 'Dragon Sunset'
7 *Pelargonium* 'Classic Scarlet' (zonal)
8 *Pelargonium* 'Dolly Varden' (variegated)

Cool and Soothing Colours

PINKS AND WHITES

Campanula isophylla
White or blue, the flowers
of this low-growing
campanula open flat, like
little saucers, and are
produced continuously
during the growing season.
A frost-hardy alternative
could be *Campanula
carpatica*, which flowers for
a shorter spell in
midsummer. The variety
'White Clips' is the best of
the whites.

Diascia rigescens
An irrepressible plant from
South Africa which roots
from cuttings in a matter of
days and grows to produce
spike after spike of pale
pink flowers. The stems are
rather lax, so the plant is
best left to flop about
informally.

Fuchsia
Because it is so easy to grow,
flowers almost constantly
with blooms of pink, white,
red and purple, and has so
many uses, this is one of the
most popular flowering
plants. When trained as
standards, fuchsias always
make good focal points, but
trailing forms are useful too,
either to blend with other
species, or to make richly
colourful hanging baskets or
window boxes on their own.

In a way, it is artificial to divide up colour schemes into hot and cool because there are so many stations in between but, in contrast to the red, orange and yellow tones, softer blues, greens, mauves and all the pastel shades can come as a welcome relief. Gentle colours, fine though they are in formal displays, work especially well among informal plantings where a harder scheme might look a little unnatural. They also make more tactful displays for distinctive surroundings. A misty scheme of silver foliage with a sparing use of soft pink flowers, for example, might enhance a rural style of house better than a display of orange marigolds.

Pale colours work especially well in poor light conditions. In northerly latitudes where evening twilight lasts a long time in summer, pallid hues, which may have looked a little washed out by day, start to come into their own at night; so if you commute a long distance or work long hours, you are likely to get more enjoyment from a border of pale colours with plenty of white flowers when you come home at night, than you would from a bed of darker hues.

OPPOSITE *In cool themes, dark foliage can enhance the effect by making the flowers look lighter. The New Guinea hybrids of* Impatiens, *whose foliage is rich purple, are a suitably brooding choice.*

LEFT *In an informal planting with bedding plants as highlights,* Impatiens *provides splashes of soft colour, and the dark blue* Salvia *'Victoria' adds interest to the foreground.*

BELOW *This could almost be a humorous interpretation of formal bedding theory. Above a haze of cheerful snowdrops, a stone cat acts as a sculptural focal point.*

THE ROLE OF FOLIAGE

Foliage makes a big contribution to soft, cool schemes. The aim with all bedding is to have dense planting with lots of vigorous growth and if the colour scheme is to be gentle, one way to bear down on intensity of hue is to step up the proportion of leaf to flower. There is nothing wrong with ordinary green foliage, indeed, if too much silver or bronze is used, natural vitality can be lost. Many flowering plants are pretty in the leaf as well. Nigellas, for example, have a lacy filigree effect; *Salvia*

ABOVE *Though it will be short-lived in flower, a bed of bearded irises makes a cool, shimmering display.*

OPPOSITE TOP *Lily-flowered tulips in soft pastels float above* Myosotis alpestris.

OPPOSITE BELOW *An ice-cold contrast of mauve petunias and ageratum, with white dahlias.*

farinacea has pretty leaves and stems as well as sombre blue flowers; and an especial favourite of mine is the richly scented heliotrope, whose foliage is dark and brooding but never obtrusive, making a beautiful contrast to silver leaves.

Imagining the effect of deep purple heliotrope dotted among pastel colours illustrates a further point about cool colours. Pale schemes are often in danger of developing an insubstantial, wishy-washy appearance with an indistinct profile. A tactful grouping of dark plants, or a band or border in a firmer colour, can bring the whole scheme together to give it form and profile.

CHOOSING COOL COLOURS

Pastel colours are represented in almost every genus. Foliage can come from silver plants such as *Helichrysum petiolare*, whose pendulous habit makes it a universal choice for containers. *Senecio cineraria* is another reliable standby where grey-leaved bedding is called for. Several hardier perennials are also valuable for foliage and these include artemisias, for silver filigree effects, and *Anaphalis*. Pelargoniums are usually thought of for hot hues, but many have pale flowers and wonderful green foliage. Ivy-leaved varieties are especially useful, making a soft, indistinct outline

where they can blend with other trailing foliage plants such as helichrysum.

Roses can be hot or cool, and a pleasant combination could be achieved with, for example, the pure white, floriferous 'Iceberg' underplanted with nothing more complicated than blue violas. These blend plenty of green leaf with the blue, even though they are constantly in bloom.

In shade or semi-shade, busy lizzies, commonplace though they may be, come in pale pink or pure clean white. Among such permanent plants as ferns and hostas, these will add floral brightness without spoiling the effect created by the natural planting.

BLUES

Agapanthus
Hybrids of these African natives make wonderful subjects for containers and bedding schemes, with cultivars ranging from pure white to deep blue. The Headbourne hybrids are said to be the hardiest.

Convolvulus sabatius
A trailing plant which grows vigorously in sunshine. The foliage has a hint of grey but the flowers, which open every day, are a soft lavender-blue shade, deepening to a purer blue as they age.

Felicia amelloides
Vigorous plants with wiry, semi-trailing stems and small, rough leaves. The flowers are produced continuously – even in winter – and are clear blue, each with a yellow centre. Frost-tender but easy to grow from cuttings, this is a perfect container plant.

Gentiana septemfida
Many gentians are easy to grow and are happy bedded out in bold, unusual groups. This form flowers from mid- to late summer, with blue trumpet flowers on stems up to 20cm (8in) high. Full light but damp, rich soil suits it best.

A Blue Scheme

Aspect and conditions: Moderately fertile, very alkaline soil, in full sun for part of the day but partially shaded by a tree to the south-west and a wall due west. The site is reasonably sheltered.

Scheme: This was planned as a formal bed. It was measured out in a circle roughly 2.5m (8ft) in diameter, and subdivided into eight sectors. The idea was to exploit different shades of blue, using dots of silver foliage and white flowers to provide gentle relief.

The bed was enclosed by a low, dark blue lavender hedge. The centre of the circle was marked with a cane pyramid, furnished with the climbing *Maurandya*: this soon covered its support and during the second half of summer produced a succession of purple-blue flowers.

Between the hedge and pyramid each sector was measured out using string and sticks radiating from the centre. The plants were counted out into equal portions and set out. Near the widest point of each sector, a small group of silver foliage alternated with a group of white impatiens. At the centre, eight white pelargoniums repeated the colour contrast. In between were massed ageratum, convolvulus and cynoglossum.

Results: The variation of blues within the scheme maintained plenty of interest. The cynoglossum had a purity of colour that tended to deepen that of the convolvulus, whose pale yellow centres added an extra dimension.

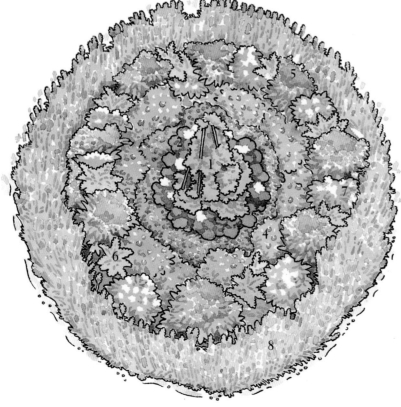

ABOVE *The natural vigour of* Convolvulus tricolor *requires it to be sited where it can spread happily.*

Plants used:

1 *Maurandya scandens* 'Jewel'
2 *Pelargonium* 'White Orbit' (raised from seed)
3 *Ageratum* 'Blue Ribbon'
4 *Convolvulus tricolor* 'Blue Ensign'
5 *Cynoglossum amabile* 'Blue Showers'
6 *Senecio* 'Silver Dust'
7 *Impatiens* 'Tempo White'
8 Lavender hedge: 'Hidcote'

SPECIAL EFFECTS

Truly creative gardeners seize every possible planting opportunity. No space, however small or limited,
is left empty, and no season, however unfriendly,
is overlooked. Bedding plants are not
merely space fillers: they are a rich
resource for creating special planting
effects. This chapter suggests schemes
for spring and autumn, foliage ideas,
and permanent plantings. It shows
how containers can be used for bedding highlights in the garden, and
offers ideas for shade and difficult
sites. Such creative bedding needs
careful planning throughout the year: beds need
to be cleared early to make way for late-summer
schemes, and bulbs must be ordered in good time
for planting in the autumn.

LEFT *Irises,* Nigella *(love-in-a-mist) and heads of* Allium
christophii *create a dreamy, early summer bedding scheme.*

ABOVE *The startling, sky-blue flowers of* Cynoglossum amabile
'Blue Showers' make an original choice for a bedding scheme.

Spring

BULBS FOR SPRING

Crocus
Large Dutch hybrids make the biggest splash: *C. vernus* 'Jeanne d'Arc' is pure white, 'Pickwick' striped purple. Smaller species of merit include *C. chrysanthus* in mauve, cream or yellow shades; and *C. tommasinianus* with frail, lilac blooms.

Iris
Early irises can herald a wider spring display. *I. reticulata* and *I. histrioïdes* will bloom in midwinter; the small yellow *I. danfordiae* is also fine.

Narcissus (small forms)
The smaller narcissus tend to be most useful in bedding schemes, because their foliage is less messy. 'Hawera' has clusters of tiny fragrant butter-coloured cups; 'Tête à Tête' has larger cups in a brighter gold.

Tulipa
Good early forms include the Fosteriana hybrids – such as 'Purissima' – and two species: *T. greigii* with bi-coloured blooms, and *T. praestans*, with multi-bloom scarlet heads. For midseason, try the Darwin hybrids, of which 'Golden Apeldoorn' is one.

Most bedding schemes are planted in late spring and removed in autumn, and it is no accident that this book dwells heavily on summer bedding. But it would be wrong to suggest that bedding is limited to any one season.

After winter, when browns and duns have depressed us in the poor daylight, we long for colour. And more than merely flowers, we will be looking for an uplifting display. A tuft of yellow crocuses or a clump of snowdrops at winter's end serve as appetizers, but what we are really after is a bedding scheme that will delight with its first flowers and then sustain a growing development of colour and form until the summer flowers are ready to take over.

Laying on such a display can be easy, even for beginners, but you do need to plan far more carefully than for any other season. Planting for spring takes place in autumn, so by summer's end you need to know which colours, shapes and moods you will want to see in six or seven months' time!

The range of herbaceous plants normally used in spring bedding displays seems somewhat restricted. This is puzzling because the choice of suitable species is vast, indeed, the only limiting factors are hardiness and flowering season. Such popular biennials as wallflowers may be unable to survive deep frosts in very cold areas, but there are plenty of suitable species that can overwinter almost anywhere. As for flowering, if spring bedding is to be stripped out and replaced with summer plants, it needs to have completed its performance a good month before the longest day. Such mid-season plants as lupins or foxgloves are therefore ruled out for early displays, but nonetheless make good interim choices, linking spring to summer.

A flowerbed planted in autumn is likely to look much the same throughout winter, so plants that are ugly or uninteresting in the dormant state need to be neutralized by species that look attractive in winter. The winter-flowering pansy flowers at its best in spring but, provided it has been raised early enough (a week or two after midsummer is the ideal sowing date), it will produce a steady though sparse supply of blooms all winter. Thus, wallflowers, which are inclined to look gawky during the short days, can be improved with an underplanting of winter pansies.

PLANTS FOR SPRING BEDDING

Apart from bulbs, popular spring plants include polyanthus primulas – coloured strains bred from wild oxlips – forget-me-nots, double daisies and drumstick primulas. But there are many bright alternatives to choose from! Honesty (*Lunaria annua*), for example, has rich magenta – or white – flowers in midspring, and attractive foliage all winter. The white-variegated form, which is more conspicuous in winter, later makes a delightful companion to dark-coloured tulips in late spring. Spring-flowering rock plants like aubrieta and rock cress (arabis) form colourful mounds in the purple-blue, pink or mauve colour range, or in white, and can be grown *en masse* in the same way as wallflowers.

In the hot colour range, there is leopard's bane (doronicums), with bright gold daisy-like flowers, and several spurges, particularly

PLANTS FOR SPRING

Brassica oleracea
Ornamental cabbages are frequently offered in seed catalogues. The colder the weather, the better the leaf colours in late winter and early spring.

Erysimum (Cheiranthus)
The biennial wallflower is widely known, but many of the perennial forms make excellent bedding. The double yellow 'Harpur Crewe' is an old variety which can be raised in large numbers from cuttings; with red tulips, or with blue winter pansies, the effect is delightful.

Primula denticulata
The drumstick primula comes in shades of lavender, purple, pink or white and produces rounded heads of flowers from strong basal rosettes. It needs moist soil.

Thermopsis montana
This non-creeping species will produce its golden-yellow, lupin-like flowers on one-year-old seedlings, and makes a pretty companion to such spring bulbs as tulips or grape hyacinths. The foliage is three-lobed and has a purplish cast.

Euphorbia polychroma which has vivid gold flowers on 30cm (1ft) stems. Low-growing alternatives to forget-me-nots include *Nemophila maculata* and several species of *Omphalodes*. Of these, the annual *O. linifolia* has grey-green, glaucous foliage followed by a froth of pearly flowers.

Fine though all these broad-leaved plants are, the mainstay of spring bedding is likely to be bulbs. Such flowers as hyacinths, tulips, fritillaries, crocuses, muscari, and, of course, narcissus, provide almost every imaginable colour. Most have interesting flower shapes and many – hyacinths and jonquils in particular – are sweetly scented.

ABOVE *A kitchen garden awaits the new season's sowing, but already it is colourful with a fine display of primroses and violets along its border.*

When planting bulbs for bedding, harmonize them with broad-leaved plants for the best effect. Tulips make natural companions for forget-me-nots. Crocuses look lovely with winter pansies especially if there are dwarf narcissus such as 'Tête à tête' or the fragrant, very late 'Bobbysoxer' to follow on. These plants make lovely bedding for underplanting shrubs, particularly roses. Once they have begun to fade, the roses will be in full leaf and summer will be on the way.

Bedding for Spring

Aspect and Conditions: A narrow border against a line of paving, set in a sunken garden that gets plenty of sun early in the year; later, trees beyond the garden cast shade. The soil is neutral and well-drained, but neither deep nor very fertile.
Scheme: The bed incorporated some permanent plants: a spreading cotoneaster, hellebores, alchemilla and *Libertia*, scruffy from winter. A spring scheme needs to capitalize on the light that reaches the garden at this time of year. Because of the uncompromising shape of the bed, repeating one plant is preferable to introducing a whole miscellany of spring-flowering material; but by using several different cultivars, interest and colour can be introduced.

The tulip is probably the most graceful and elegant of the spring-flowering bulbs. Somehow its erect carriage and fleshy petals help it to carry off some of the brashest of flower colours, and boldest of stripes and speckles, without ever looking vulgar. The varieties used here are particularly choice: 'Union Jack', is a deep rich pink, and makes a good partner to 'Attila', striped pink and white; 'Oranje Nassau' has a blood-red, flame-flecked, double flower. At this time of year, colour is so welcome that clashing colours can be used together with impunity.
Results: A lively and cheerful spring display, with frothing forget-me-nots and mixed polyanthus for contrast.

ABOVE *There are so many fine cultivars of tulip that it can be difficult to choose between them.* 'Garden Party' *can usually be relied on for a display year after year, even if left* in situ.

Plants used:

1   *Tulipa* 'Golden Melody'
2   *Libertia grandiflora*
3   *Tulipa* 'Union Jack'
4   *Tulipa* 'Attila'
5   *Tulipa* 'Aladdin' with
    T. 'Oranje Nassau'
6   *Polyanthus*
7   *Helleborus foetidus*
8   *Tulipa* 'Queen of Sheba'
9   *Tulipa* 'Garden Party'
10 *Helleborus foetidus*
11 *Tulipa* 'Arie Alkemade's Memory'
12 *Libertia grandiflora*
13 *Tulipa* 'Meissner Porzellan'
14 *Myosotis alpestris*

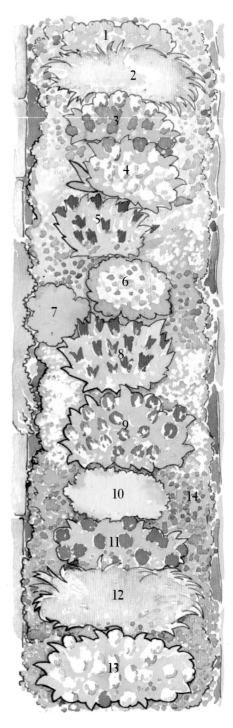

Autumn Specials

PLANTS FOR AUTUMN

Aster
The tall *A. novae-angliae* hybrids are mildew-resistant and make useful background material to autumn displays. But finest of all is *A. lateriflorus*, which carries its colour deep into winter.

Dendranthema
Chrysanthemums are mainstays of autumn schemes. The spray varieties are most resilient, and of these the Korean forms score highly. Old favourites like 'Clara Curtis' (single pink), 'Duchess of Edinburgh' (blood red) and 'Anastasia' (pink) are still good subjects.

Rudbeckia
Offers warm colours running from rich mahogany to searing yellow, on huge daisy flowers with intriguing dark centres. The series 'Marmalade', in cool yellow, and the perennial varieties 'Goldsturm' and 'Goldquelle' are the best for bedding.

Sedum
S. spectabile and *S. telephium* provide cool green or grey foliage all summer, then pink, rusty red or creamy-coloured flowers all autumn.

The garden's most colourful interlude comes with summer's end, when dusty midday heat is tempered by cool nights and heavy dews. Autumn foliage is on the turn and short-day plants are reaching their flowering climax. Most bedding plants move into a declining phase at this time but it is possible to extend the season deep into autumn by choosing the right species.

There are two distinct approaches to autumn bedding. One is to set aside an area for the exclusive use of plants which only flower at the back end of the year. This is fine if your garden can accommodate such a border without this making it dull at other times.

The alternative is to include some autumn-flowering plants among summer bedding.

Dahlias and dendranthemas (chrysanthemums) contribute much to the autumn flora. Dahlias come in all colours except clean blue. There are strident reds, soft lemons, warm salmons, cool mauves and rich purples. Flower size varies from tiny, rounded 'pompons' to huge 'decoratives' that look like wedding hats. Flower shape varies, too, and includes flattened 'water lily' blooms and elegant, spiky 'cactus' dahlias. Plant stature also varies, from low-growing bedding types, usually raised from seed, to tall exhibition cultivars. Dahlia tubers must be lifted at the end of autumn and stored frost free. The plants can be multiplied by division or from basal cuttings and are resistant to most diseases except virus, which disfigures the plants. Once infected, the stock should be discarded.

Dendranthemas are almost as diverse as dahlias, but are more versatile. Their colours are softer, and more comfortable in mixed plantings. Furthermore, outdoor varieties are frost hardy and can be left in the ground for years, although they do benefit from regular division. They are easy to raise from basal cuttings (page 39). Spray varieties work best outdoors, standing up well to autumn winds.

OPPOSITE AND RIGHT *The warm tones of coleus foliage (opposite top) are absolutely right for the season, and often at their best when the flowers of dendranthemas open. Asters (left) provide an eruption of autumn colour. Most exciting of all is this pairing (right) of the blowzy* Colchicum *with long-flowering* Tagetes

Foliage

With bedding, we use plant material as a kind of furnishing textile and in this respect foliage can be used on its own. But we also need to consider the role foliage can play as a support for floral displays, enhancing colour here, toning it down there; contrasting light colours with dark here, harmonizing and blending different hues there.

When considering foliage as supporting material, it is important to think of the bedding scheme as a whole. Plant for textures, shapes and colours first, and then look for plants which best match the style you have devised, feathery and fluffy perhaps, or bold and broad. Colour differences in foliage tend to be subtle and more muted than among flowers, so even such sharply contrasting hues as the bright green of, say, kochia planted with the silvery laciness of *Centaurea gymnocarpa* or *Senecio viravira* are still far gentler in

their effect than would be flowers of a different colour. This means that the result of using lots of foliage in a mixed scheme will be to soften, tone down and to make transitions between colours easier on the eye. Colours that might be quite uncomfortable together can be held apart, but at the same time conjoined in sympathetic hues and textures by integrating them with foliage. We have already seen how hard colours can be softened with silvery leaves (page 51) but in fact all strong colours benefit from a backing of foliage. Above all, though, when making your selection, it is worth reminding yourself that green goes with everything.

Foliage can also be used to make a strong statement in a soft colour scheme. Being architectural in their outline as well as bold in their colours, dot plants such as the purple-leaved cordyline, dark cannas, the rusty leaved *Ricinus communis* 'Impala' or vivid green banana plants (*Ensete ventricosum*) provide a strong focus to bedding.

Foliage on its own needs different treatment but it is perfectly feasible to arrange a bed with plants selected for foliage only. Using such brightly coloured varieties as flame nettle (*Coleus* or *Solenostemon*), spider plants (*Chlorophytum*), amaranthus, senecio and iresine, you can achieve an effect almost as colourful as a floral display. But foliage can do so much more than merely mimic flowers. In natural plantings, for instance, the tall permanent shrubs and trees may be so handsome in their own right that all they need is a little green furnishing at their bases. A simple ground cover of such perennials as *Geranium*

OPPOSITE A *judicious choice of foliage and a handsome textural contrast as well. Broad-leaved hostas make a foil for the feathery silver foliage of* Artemisia 'Powys Castle', *while lobelia and blue delphiniums add cool flower colours.*

LEFT A *group of tender echeverias makes unusual foliage bedding at the feet of shrubs and herbaceous plants. They create their own focal point in soft grey tones.*

macrorrhizum or pulmonarias would work perfectly well here but, if you wanted to achieve an effect quickly, or if you wanted to make changes each year, leafy temporary bedding could provide the answer. Much of this would blend cheerfully with more permanent ground cover – indeed, it is hard to decide which is bedding and which ground cover – but it has the advantage of rapid development and changeability. This technique is especially useful in newly planted borders, enabling you to beef up permanent ground cover by filling gaps with bedding. Temporary plants for such

uses include golden feverfew, ornamental brassicas – especially those in soft greeny pinks rather than garish creams – and ornamental grasses. The green flowers of *Moluccella laevis* (bells of Ireland), or *Nicotiana langsdorffii* and some of its green-flowered tobacco hybrids, all have a similar effect to foliage but, because they are flowers, provide a little extra visual interest.

In formal gardens, especially where there are such structures as dividing walls, steps, terraces and so on, or where there are clipped hedges, foliage makes a soothing alternative

RIGHT Golden foliage is perfect for brightening warm colour themes and will associate with most colours, including the pinkish red of these verbenas, grown in containers to create a change of height. The gold form of Helichrysum petiolare is a good-natured trailer which thrives in the hot dry conditions of this terrace.

OPPOSITE LEFT Dark foliage can both tone down a colour scheme and add rich highlights. Here, golden flowers are made to look even brighter by a row of dark ornamental beet behind. Meanwhile, its sombre note separates the bright foreground from the more subdued planting at the back.

OPPOSITE RIGHT A strong contrast between warm and cool colour using nothing but foliage. The silver leaves of Senecio 'Silver Dust' shine out brightly against a collection of plants with brooding purple leaves.

PURPLES AND BRONZES

Amaranthus tricolor 'Joseph's Coat'
The young leaves are bronze, but as this tender annual matures the leaf colour heightens to exhibit golden streaks and stipples against a red background. Colours are brightest when the plants are grown in a hot, sunny position. The related *Amaranthus caudatus* (love-lies-bleeding) has red tassel flowers.

Canna imperialis (Indian shot plant)
In cold climates, these are more frequently used as dot plants for their foliage rather than as massed bedding. When planted in drifts, their combination of broad, gleaming leaves and vivid flowers makes them a perfect choice. Flower colours range through red and orange to deep or pale yellow against bright green or brooding purple foliage.

Lobelia cardinalis
The purple-bronze foliage of this species makes a bold statement on its own, but in late summer tall spires of vivid scarlet flowers create a breathtaking contrast with the leaves. A moisture-loving plant which needs rich soil.

to flowers. Permanent low, clippable shrubs can be put to good use here, adding an extra layer and enhancing the overall design and structure. Low-growing laurels such as *Prunus laurocerasus* 'Otto Luyken', dull though they may sound, are anything but, forming banks of glossy evergreen foliage with the annual bonus of a crop of white blossoms. Bergenias flower in spring, too, but are essentially foliage plants with a uniquely leathery texture to their leaves, many of which turn bronze in cold weather.

Hardy herbaceous plants that make good ground cover often make good bedding as well. Be warned, however, that many are invasive! The decorative deadnettles (*Lamium maculatum*), produce a constant run of fresh foliage that makes them lovely for growing as part of both spring and summer schemes. My own personal preference is for white blooms and, of these, *L. maculatum* 'White Nancy' has the prettiest leaves of silver, edged with green; another firm favourite is the white-flowered form of campion, *Lychnis coronaria* 'Alba', with its tall, ghostly grey foliage. Lady's mantle (*Alchemilla mollis*), has decorative foliage which, when it rains, collects a pearly drop of water in the centre of each leaf; and it seeds copiously.

This is merely a handful of suggestions. Since all green plants have leaves, the opportunities for experimenting with foliage are almost infinite, so why not be brave and try something different?

Edible Schemes

Edible bedding is far more than a fanciful notion, indeed most food production is raised with the bedding technique. A potager is, in essence, nothing more than a fancy bedding scheme using food plants partly as decoration and partly as a source of raw materials for the kitchen. So if you want to grow food but have limited space, why not set out a small bedding scheme of edible plants? With so many different leaf types, colouring and growth habits among vegetables, you could make it look ornamental as well as being productive. Planting and planning procedure will be exactly as with any other bedding – all that is different is the choice of plants.

Most of the interest will arise from differences in foliage textures and colours. Ferny green carrot leaves, for example, contrast with the broader, glaucous, leathery leaves of cabbages or broccoli. Ornamental cabbages are an obvious choice but, if they are healthy and well grown, culinary kinds have their own beauty. Tightly curled kale, resembling giant parsley, adds another texture, and looks pleasing behind the spiky foliage of leeks or onions. Strongly coloured leaves will help here, too, so rather than spinach, you could plant rhubarb chard – which tastes just as good – for its brilliant red stems and dark leaves.

Salad plants, especially those with lengthy cropping periods, are useful. Lettuce varieties like 'Little Leprechaun' or 'Lollo Rosso', the leaves of which you can pick a few at a time, are the best choice. Chives are useful because they too can be cut and will grow again.

For height, you could make a centrepiece of climbing beans on a wigwam. Many varieties

OPPOSITE *The bright tones of ornamental cabbages make an unusual choice as bedding for this formal scheme, with an ornamental pear tree providing the focal point.*

LEFT *Bright nasturtium flowers associate well with the scarlet stems of rhubarb chard.*

BELOW *A colourful collection of culinary sage plants, kept well trimmed to ensure that there is plenty of fresh new growth.*

have flower colours from white to pink to red or purple. Summer colour is also easy to enhance with outdoor tomatoes, especially varieties which produce successions of small fruits. In warm areas, aubergines and red chillies can be effective, but should be started off under glass and planted mature. Nasturtiums are another good choice, not only for the brightness of their edible flowers, but because their seeds can be pickled to make an intriguing substitute for capers.

Herbs add extra interest. Sages, thymes and oreganos come in a variety of golden, purple and variegated forms, all of which are perfect for a beautiful, edible bedding scheme as most of their flavours are as good as those of the common green forms.

Edible Bedding

Aspect and conditions: The site has deep rich soil, inclined to be heavy. It is in sun, but is sheltered to the west by a high hedge and is therefore in shadow after mid-afternoon.

Scheme: A rectangular plot measuring 3.5m (12ft) by 2m (7ft) provided enough space for an attractive display and also modest supplies of fresh food.

Structure for the scheme came from a pair of simple trellis pyramids, which provided support for climbing beans and for the traditional, highly scented sweet pea. The pyramids can be made easily from four pieces of ordinary fan-shaped trellis, wired together. At the centre of the plot I placed a decorative cloche. The edges of the area were marked out with clippable plants of thyme and the remaining space was filled with a patch-work of leafy vegetables. These were trimmed regularly to keep them within narrow bounds, and the trimmings could be cooked and eaten.

Colour came from ornamental cab-bages. These were sown out of season, in spring, and were therefore much more gently coloured than if they had been raised at the normal time in autumn, when winter frost would guarantee much stronger hues.

Results: The 'potager' made a lively dis-play which, though it needed constant attention, provided great pleasure and amusement. With steady replacement of crops as they are eaten, such a scheme could run continuously.

ABOVE As *summer advances the cloche becomes redundant, but it can stay in place to make a decorative centrepiece amidst the ornamental cabbages.*

Plants used:
1   Ornamental cabbage 'White Christmas'
2   Domestic cabbage
3   Carrot
4   *Lathyrus odoratus* and runner bean
5   Rhubarb chard
6   French marigold and shallot
7   Ornamental cabbages 'Pink Beauty' and 'Rose Bouquet'
8   Spinach
9   Culinary sage
10 *Thymus* 'Silver Posie'
11 Garlic chives

Permanent Bedding

PERMANENT PLANTS

Crambe maritima
Seakale is a pretty plant which produces generous mounds of hairless grey-green foliage and sprays of scented white flowers in early summer. The plants are easy to multiply by root cuttings or simply by division, but once established the roots are persistent.

Sphaeralcea munroana
Woody perennials with a creeping habit and deep green foliage. Every leaf axil carries a single, coral-pink flower. It is easily grown from cuttings and flowers for the whole of the growing season. In mild areas this mallow relative will survive year after year, but elsewhere protect the roots in winter or take cuttings as a precaution.

Viola (pansies, violas and violettas)
Because they germinate in cool soil, members of this genus can be used as self-generating colonies. They are fully hardy and can bridge the gap between the main bedding seasons. Pansies and violas should be dead-headed and pinched back regularly to keep them flowering.

Much of our discussion of plants has revolved around the routine spring and autumn rituals of stripping out old plants then bedding out new ones for the two main seasons. But much bedding – besides mere ground cover – can be either partly or wholly permanent. Roses, for example, provide the perfect anchor for a blend of seasonal and permanent planting. Among large-flowered modern roses 'Just Joey' (salmon apricot) is one of the most dependable, and for smaller plants, look for patio roses such as 'Royal Salute' (pink). The typical rose garden or border might consist of shrub roses planted with an element of formality so that, as well as looking attractive, they are easy to get at to prune and spray. Such beds would be dull, especially when the roses are neither in flower nor leaf, without imaginative underplanting.

Spring bulbs are especially useful as permanent bedding in rose gardens – or anywhere else, for that matter – and, if planted deeply enough, can remain in the ground undisturbed regardless of frequent replanting above them. When selecting bulbs, bear in mind the colour of emerging rose foliage – often a liverish copper-red – and match flowers accordingly.

There is no need to consider the rose colours out of season, of course, but if your design calls for a strict adherence to that specific colour scheme, spring bedding under roses can achieve this easily. In the home of my childhood, my mother planted pink and white roses – 'Dearest' and 'Iceberg' – in two borders that flanked a path. In spring she replicated the formula using the tulips 'Clara Butt' and 'White Triumphator'.

All lavenders are a splendid choice for permanent bedding. Their silver-grey foliage looks lively in winter and is a useful foil for bright spring flowers. Lavender blossom, as well as being attractive to bees and butterflies, forms drifts of colour which blend with the sultry hues of summer. Several varieties go on producing flowers right through to the frosts if they are cut back after their main flush. There are other shrubs which behave like lavender, though few are as dependable. Cotton lavender (*Santolina*), is a useful bedding shrublet that needs cutting hard back immediately after flowering. The pale forms are the easiest to harmonize with other bedding, and of these *Santolina neapolitana* has grey foliage and lemon flowers; but *S. rosmarinifolia* 'Primrose Gem' is perhaps better for contrasting with lavender because its foliage is deep emerald and its flowers pale yellow. Sixteenth-century gardeners loved germander (*Teucrium* × *lucidrys*) and with good reason. The foliage is glossy and evergreen but the flowers are a rich pink. Germander, though technically a shrub, fares best if cut to ground level after flowering.

Herbaceous perennial bedding offers almost limitless scope. Obviously the wisest choices will be of plants that flower over a long period. Penstemons are unsurpassable in this respect, and narrow-leaved kinds such as the pink 'Evelyn' and ruby-red 'Garnet' are surprisingly hardy. The temptation is to grow mixtures of these stately plants, but groups of the same variety are more effective. Imagine a permanent bed bordered by the deep purple-blue *Lavandula angustifolia* 'Hidcote' and

containing rich pink penstemons for summer, underplanted with a mix of the green-and-pink tulip 'Greenland' with forget-me-nots scattered among the dormant penstemons for spring. In winter, groups of Dutch crocus could relieve the monotony of the foliage – pure white 'Jeanne d'Arc' perhaps, or the purple-and-white striped 'Pickwick'. That lot would ensure a sumptuous bedding display for all seasons.

In beds where you intend to replant twice each year, it is often worth siting anchor plants to act as permanent structural centrepieces or high spots. Remaining constant with all the change that is going on around them, these help to create a feeling of continuity. A single, well-shaped shrub, plumb in the middle of a small bed, for instance, is enough to make an anchor. A clipped holly, perhaps, or a camellia gently pruned to keep a reasonable shape, would work well. Bay loves to be shaped and it is possible to buy, at a price, bay trees ready trained into spirals, pyramids, domes or bobbles.

Simple statements in otherwise dull spots of the garden also lend themselves to permanent bedding. A long, tall hedge may be too beautiful a feature to clutter with fussy underplanting, especially a venerable yew or holly hedge, but could be enhanced with something simple and monochromatic. I remember seeing, in an old English garden, a long grass path bordered by a yew hedge along the base of which grew a single line of catmint (Nepeta sibirica). Its simple, blue flowers contrasted with the dark yew, increasing the sense of drama.

ABOVE AND LEFT *Although the bulk of our bedding schemes are replanted at least once a year, plants like roses and heathers are perfect subjects for displays that can run year after year.*

Containers

In spite of their space restrictions, containers have a great deal going for them when it comes to bedding. Container culture uses purpose-made composts and enables plants to be nurtured to their own special requirements. Pots and troughs can be moved about, enabling changes to be made as and when required, which is about as near to instant gardening as you can get! But above all, the right containers can make the plants growing in them look even more beautiful than they might do in the ground.

To work in the same way as bedding or to support bedding schemes, containers should be planned to harmonize with each other. The rule that simplicity works best and that limited numbers of colours carry the most

impact applies as much to container culture as to any other kind of bedding. An urn or a large tub, for instance, set in a traditional flowerbed makes a delightful focal point. A strong colour scheme might work well, as might an architectural plant with foliage that is strikingly different to that of the surrounds, but the colours must not clash nor the style be at variance with the rest of the planting. Stand out as it does, the container is still part of a larger scheme.

The other important point about containers is that since they elevate their contents above ground level, they provide an opportunity to use pendulous plants, softening but not hiding their outline. For example, the simple act of planting a couple of ivies to grace the sides of a large pot holding a single shrub makes a big difference. Trailing plants that are more colourful and develop more rapidly than ivies – and there are dozens – are useful for summer displays.

Containers can be grouped to create an entire garden wherever there is an absence of soil or where space is limited, and the bedding style used to bind together an otherwise disparate batch of pots to create a feeling of wholeness. Even when different plants are used, it helps to run a linking theme through all of them. Thus, even though you may have planted as diverse a mix as, say, fuchsias, jalapa, morning glories, geraniums, lilies and evergreen shrubs in your containers, pale blue trailing lobelia or *Helichrysum petiolare* in each container will help to bring the collection together without spoiling the overall effect or losing the diversity.

The Challenging Site

Mimulus guttatus
In damp shade, the monkey or musk flowers will produce highly coloured blooms and lush foliage. Easily grown from seed, many strains have bright chestnut, coppery red or orange markings on the flowers as well as the more usual yellow. Worth seeking out are 'Andean Nymph', (pink and primrose), and *M. cupreus* 'Whitecroft Scarlet'.

Impatiens
Busy lizzies are especially good at coping with moderate shade. The paler forms and pure whites are more likely to show up well in the gloom than are red or dark flowered forms. There are also double forms.

Hosta
More frequently used as hardy perennials, hostas lend themselves well to permanent formal bedding.

Lamium maculatum
Garden forms of this deadnettle include silver-leaved, green and golden forms. Easy to propagate – just tear shoots off the main plants and push them into the ground where they will root – this makes almost instant bedding for shade.

Most gardening difficulties are bigger in theory than in reality: the limitations of a site are more likely to be spectres haunting the gardener's mind than actual problems. The first task of any creative planter, therefore, is to match the plant to the surroundings. This must include practical and cultural considerations as well as what will look right.

Having struck a positive note, it would be silly to suggest that every square centimetre of the garden will look glorious all the time. Some spots will need more careful planning than others and have less potential but, when you consider the vast number of plant species in cultivation, it becomes clear that however uncompromising the conditions there are likely to be plants that will thrive there.

Common difficulties are caused by excesses of shade, drought, cold, heat, poor soil and wind. The first task, therefore, is to assess the gravity of these drawbacks and to see how many of them can be alleviated. Soil is easy to improve with composts and feeding, and to make alkaline with additions of lime. It is less easy to make soil acid, but sprinkling flowers of sulphur helps. Shelter is seldom difficult to create, either by planting or by erecting screens and fences. Shedding light into shade is trickier, especially if your garden is in the shadow of a large building, but trees can be trimmed and thinned to let in more light.

Having done as much as possible to alleviate the problems, the next step is to select the right plants for the conditions. **Shade** is

ABOVE LEFT *Nicotianas are a dependable bedding plant in areas with poor soil, and most forms will do acceptably well in light shade.*

OPPOSITE *Creating a bedding display in shade is quite a challenge, yet this is a very common condition, particularly in town gardens. Impatiens are perfect for moderate light conditions, where their flower colours will glow brightly all summer. They will do less well in burning sunlight, and, conversely, very dense shade.*

BELOW LEFT *Problem areas in a garden can transform to planting opportunities with the right choice of bedding plant. In a boggy spot, where both drainage and light quality are poor, mimulus or monkey flowers may well perform where other bedding fails.*

probably the toughest challenge, with exposure running a close second. Extreme shade may preclude the bedding of anything but the toughest ferns – the hart's tongue fern (*Asplenium scolopendrium*), or *Dryopteris filix-mas* – or perhaps a ground cover of ivy. A little more light should allow you to grow primulas for spring and impatiens for summer – white varieties show up best in gloom. Variegated foliage can be especially useful in shade and such plants as *Tolmiea menziesii* 'Taff's Gold' or the cream-and-green *Symphytum grandiflorum* 'Variegatum' grow and spread rapidly, even though they are really ground cover plants rather than bedders.

Exposed spots, as long as they are in full light, call for tough, vigorous plants. Large leaves could be blown to shreds and tall, spindly plants could be rocked in the wind or

FOR EXPOSED SITES

*Argyranthemum
foeniculaceum*
Foliage and flower are of
equal value in this ideal
container plant. The finely
divided, glaucous foliage
makes a pleasing foil for the
single, white, daisy flowers,
which appear all summer.
Tolerant of low water levels
and quick to regenerate
itself if damaged by wind.

Calendula
One of the easiest of the
hardy annuals. Most forms
have bright orange or
yellow, rayed flowers which
are good for cutting as well
as for bedding. The stems
are aromatic and the foliage
green and healthy-looking.
Sow some seed in autumn
and over-winter the young
plants for some large
specimens; then re-sow in
spring for continuity. They
look ravishing with pure
blue cornflowers.

Pelargonium peltatum
The familiar ivy-leaved
geranium. Vigorous
varieties such as the Swiss
'Balcon' series and the
smaller, more compact
'mini-cascade' have tended
to supersede earlier forms,
because their stems are less
likely to be damaged by
wind.

ABOVE *The base of a high wall is often both
shaded and dry. Permanent plants like hostas
will survive in such conditions, and can be
brightened up for summer with impatiens.*

LEFT ABOVE AND LEFT *Hot, dry conditions with
thin soil that bakes in summer may prove
challenging to most plants but there is still
plenty of bedding that will cope.
Mesembryanthemums or Livingstone daisies
are perfect for hot, dry conditions, and need sun
to open their blooms (left top). Petunias are
resilient but better still, for hot spots, are
sedums or colourful portulacas (left).*

Hardy annuals make a dashing alternative, not only for exposed sites but also for **thin, rapidly-draining soils**. They can be direct sown and they germinate surprisingly quickly. As long as food and water are supplied, they are capable of creating a stunning effect at great speed. Cornflowers, larkspurs, nigella, candytuft and calendula are all foolproof seed-raised plants which give months of service. Pansies and violas are useful here too, seeding around with abandon.

For **hot, dry sites** that bake in summer, petunias are the obvious choice. Their wide colour range and resilience, especially in drought, has made them a worldwide favourite. Being a lover of strong colours, I delight in the California poppy with its bright orange, yellow or salmon flowers, which make an exciting contrast with the cobalt-blue of annual lupins. Most of these annuals have the merit of self-seeding obligingly and need never be replaced once the first packet has been purchased!

Site problems occur by degrees, and each garden is unique with its own special environment. It is best, therefore, to allow the plants to tell you whether they enjoy their home or not. By trial and error, and even with the sketchiest of plant knowledge, you will soon learn which species are likely to adapt well to the environment you can offer. Those that thrive can be planted again; others, which take exception to their treatment, can be abandoned. With perennials or fancy shrubs, this 'hit or miss' approach would soon turn into an expensive game, but with almost all temporary plants you can experiment year after year at relatively little cost. Cheapness and versatility is, after all, one of the main joys of bedding!

even knocked over. Low-growing plants such as French marigolds, ageratum and the ubiquitous lobelia, commonplace though they are, will perform well in surprisingly adverse conditions. If they are well fed, with regular watering at the beginning of the season to help them kick off to a vigorous start, they will create a measure of shelter within their own beds as they grow. If yellow and orange shades are anathema to you, try some of the new, compact, seed-raised pelargoniums. The modern dwarf series are big on flower power and keep their heads low enough to escape the worst of the winds.

FOR HOT, DRY SITES

Dianthus (Pinks)
A broad genus including border pinks and sweet williams (*Dianthus barbatus*), both of which can be used as permanent bedding. Border pinks persist for several years and are easy to multiply from cuttings taken in midsummer. Sweet williams grow readily from seed and will self-sow, if left undisturbed in a sunny bed.

Eschscholzia californica
A hardy annual that will germinate and flower in a few weeks. The species is bright orange, making a fine contrast with the blue-grey of the foliage, but there are good colour strains available from creamy yellow to salmon pink. A sun lover which thrives in poor soil.

Portulaca
Pretty, low-growing plants with succulent foliage and brightly coloured flowers with silky petals, produced steadily through the summer. They perform best in hot, dry conditions and flower most profusely on sunny days. Easy to raise from seed and ideal for a spot too dry for most bedding.

Plant Directory

Listed in this Directory are the most common bedding plants that the gardener is likely to grow. The symbols indicate the basic cultivation information for each plant; special notes on growing or propagating are added at the end of the entry.

Key to Symbols

Types of Plant:
TS   tender shrub
HP   hardy perennial
HHA   half hardy annual
TP   tender perennial
B   bulb
HB   hardy biennial

Aspect:
☼   sun
✹   shade
◐   light shade

Soil:
□   dry
≋   moist
●   any

Season of interest:
❁   spring
✿   summer
✇   autumn
✳   winter

Propagation:
▒   seed
♈   cuttings
◪   division

Note: heights given are approximate, based on averages for the whole group.

ABUTILON
TS ☼ ● ✿/✇ ♈

To 2m/6ft or more but easy to keep pruned to any size. Shrubs often used as dot plants with decorative foliage and colourful flowers. 'Ashford Red' and 'Canary bird' have green leaves; A. pictum thompsonii is variegated, A. x suntense has mauve blossom.
● Easy to raise from cuttings taken in summer. Pinch back to promote bushy growth.

AGERATUM
HHA ☼ ● ✿ ▒

15–45cm/6in–1½ft. Produces flowers in small blue puffs. Good F1 hybrids include 'Blue Ribbon' and 'Blue Swords', both dwarf. Taller growing kinds include 'Tall Blue'.
● Dislikes poor soil but tolerates hot weather. Sow seed in heat in late winter, feeding young plants well for bushy growth before planting out.

AMARANTHUS Love-lies-bleeding
HHA/Ha ☼/◐ ● ✿ ▒

30–60cm/1–2ft. Flowering forms have red tassels; foliage species come in bronze colours which brighten up best in full sun. 'Amar Kiran' and 'Joseph's Coat' are good for foliage; flowering kinds include 'Red Fox' or A. caudatus.
● Sow in early spring, indoors or out, but watch for slugs which devour young plants.

ANTIRRHINUM Snapdragon
TP grown as HHA ☼ ● ✿ ▒

15–60cm/6in–2ft. Almost frost-hardy perennials with snapdragon blooms in all colours except blue. Dwarf kinds include 'Magic Carpet' or 'Dwarf Trumpet Serenade'. Medium-sized varieties include 'Monarch Mixed', 'F1 Coronette' and 'Lipstick Gold F2 Hybrid'.
● Susceptible to rust. Sow indoors in midwinter to plant out in spring. Remove faded spikes to ensure further flowers.

ARGYRANTHEMUM Marguerites
TP ☼ ● ✿/✇ ♈/▒

45cm/1½ft or more. Branched, lax perennials, therefore good in containers. Rayed, daisy flowers in pink, white, apricot or yellow shades. Varieties include 'Mary Wootton' (pink), 'Jamaica Primrose' and 'Peach Cheeks'. 'Chelsea Girl' has filigree foliage.
● Easy from cuttings, which need pinching back regularly to promote bushy growth. Some varieties need supporting.

ARTEMISIA Wormwood
HP/TP/TS ☼ □ ❁/✿/✇ ♈

Dwarf to 60cm/2ft or more. Silver foliage, often filigree, with a wiry, shrubby habit. A. 'Lambrook Silver' has lacy foliage, A. ludoviciana produces solid, silvery leaves.
● They thrive in drought and will suffer under very wet conditions.

BEGONIA
TP grown as HHA ☼/◐ ● ✿ ▒/◪ ♈

15–60cm/6in–2ft or more. Huge group consisting of two main types:
Tuberous-rooted kinds have big, bright flowers, fleshy stems and vivid green foliage. Upright forms include 'Nonstop' series (F1) but 'Chanson' mixed have a pendulous habit making them ideal for hanging baskets and containers.
Begonia semperflorens is grown as much for the green or bronze foliage as for blooms. Good varieties include 'Olympia' series, with green foliage and red, pink or white flowers and 'Coco' series for darker foliage.
● Tuberous-rooted types can be started in spring with bottom heat, or plants can be raised from seed or cuttings.
● Sow Semperflorens types in late winter at 20–25°C/68–75°F. Young plants must not go cooler than 15°C/42°F. Can be difficult to grow from seed, but many suppliers now offer plugs of young plants.

BELLIS
HP ☼ ● ❁ ▒/◪

To 15cm/6in. Dwarf plants with 'tufty' flowers in white or pastel shades but with dark pink or red edges to petals. Varieties include 'Rose Carpet' and 'White Carpet' or the mixture 'Spring Star Mixed', or 'Habanera'.
● Best results when raised from seed sown during the summer and planted out in autumn for spring bloom.

BIDENS

TP ○/◑ ● ✿ ▨

45–60cm/1½–2ft. Trailing plants for containers. Produces yellow flowers in a mist of lacy foliage. 'Golden Goddess' is one of the best forms.
● Slug damage likely in early stages, so plant in good growing conditions.

BRACHYCOME Swan River daisy

HHA ○ ● ✿ ▨

To 20cm/8in. Pendulous habit, feathery foliage and purple flowers make this a fine container plant. The species *B. iberidiifolia* is pretty, good named forms are 'Blue Star' and 'White Splendour'.
● Sow seed indoors, early. Feed regularly to lengthen flowering season.

BRASSICA Cabbage

HB ○/◑ ● ✂/◨/❉ ▨

Ornamental kinds seldom develop hearts, forming coloured rosettes instead. But all cabbage can be ornamental! Mixtures include 'Ornamental Mixed'. Self-coloured series include 'Pink Beauty', 'White Christmas' and 'Rose Bouquet'.
● Sow in late summer for winter displays or in spring for summer use (spring-sown plants may bolt in hot weather). Feed liberally when young and watch for caterpillar damage.

CALCEOLARIA

HHA/TP ○ ● ✿ ▨/◨/⚘

30–60cm/1–2ft. Subshrubs or herbaceous with strange, bag-like flowers produced over long periods. For bedding, herbaceous series include 'Sunset Mixed', but for dot plants or containers the shrubby yellow *C. integrifolia* is dependable.
● Shrubs are best raised from cuttings taken the previous summer. Plant with care in a sheltered position to protect fragile wood.

CALENDULA Pot Marigold

HA ○ ● ✂/◨ ▨

30–45cm/1–1½ft. Rugged growers with rayed flowers in orange to yellow range and with aromatic foliage. The 'Gitana' series have dark petal-edges; 'Orange King' has large blooms.
● Sow seed outdoors in autumn for extra large plants. Re-sow in monthly succession for sustained blooming.

CANNA Indian Shot Plant

TP ○ ●/≋ ✿ ◨

60cm–1.2m/2–4ft. Bold foliage and bright flowers are produced freely in warm countries. Most varieties are raised vegetatively – look for 'Lucifer' (dark leaves) and 'Assault' (scarlet flowers). 'Tropical Rose' comes true from seed.
● Protect roots over winter months or bring whole plants indoors.

CENTAUREA Cornflower

HA ○ ● ✿ ▨

15cm–1m/6in–3ft. Silvery foliage and flowers with waisted seed capsules. 'Blue Diadem' is dependable and best for cutting. Dwarf kinds include 'Ultra Dwarf' and 'Polka Dot', which come in blue, pink or white.
● Sow outdoors in autumn or spring. Thin to 20cm/8in apart.

CHEIRANTHUS Wallflower

HB ○ ●/☐ ✂ ▨/⚘

30–60cm/1–1½ft. Fragrant, bushy, many-coloured and easy to grow. 'Vulcan' is blood red and grows tall; 'Scarlet Bedder' and 'Primrose Bedder' are compact; 'Tom Thumb Mixed' are dwarf.
● Sow seed in early summer for following spring and plant out in autumn. Firm in well: when top leaves are tweaked, the leaves should break off before the plants come out of the ground.
● Perennial kinds can be grown from cuttings taken in midsummer.

COLEUS Flame nettle

TP ○/◑ ● ✿ ▨/⚘

30cm–1m/1–3ft. Vivid leaf colour and vigorous growth in ideal conditions. Varieties include 'Dragon Sunset' (dark, frilled foliage) and trailing 'Scarlet Poncho'.
● Easily grown from seed sown in heat in spring, or from cuttings. Susceptible to cool weather early in season so plant out late.

CONVOLVULUS Bindweed

HP/TP/HA ○ ● ✿ ▨/◨

15–30cm/6in–1ft. Saucer-shaped flowers produced all summer.
● The perennial *C. sabatius* divides readily but needs frost protection.

CORDYLINE

TS ○ ● ✂/◨/◨ ◨

To 6m/20ft but used smaller in bedding. Dot plants with spiky leaves and upright habit. Named forms include 'Purpurea' with dark leaves and 'Variegata'.
● In cold areas, they must be brought indoors during the winter. Can be kept in containers all year round.

COSMOS

HHA/TP ○ ● ✿ ▨/⚘

To 1m/3ft or more. Feathery foliage and flowers in clean colours of pink or white. The perennial *C. atrosanguineus* smells of chocolate and has deep maroon flowers. Annual mixtures include 'Sensation' mixed. 'Sonata' is a superb white and 'Sea Shells' have tubular petals.
● Can be direct sown outdoors, or pot raised. Perennial kinds best grown from cuttings.

CROCUS

B ○/◑ ● ✂ ◨ (corms)

To 10cm/4in. Vast range of dwarf bulbs, autumn planted to flower in late winter or early spring. Dutch hybrids include white 'Jeanne d'Arc' and striped 'Pickwick'. *C. tommasinianus* and *C. chrysanthus* are good smaller species.
● Cormlets can be transplanted to hasten their spread. Watch for rodent damage.

CYNOGLOSSUM

HA ○/◑ ● ✿ ▨

30cm/1ft. Vivid blue forget-me-not flowers are produced over many weeks. 'Blue Showers' is the best of the blues but there is also a white form, 'Avalanche'.
● The large seeds can be direct sown or raised under cover before planting out. Feed well in early stages to develop large plants.

DAHLIA

TP ○ ● ✿/◨ ▨/◨/⚘

20cm–1.5m/8in–5ft. A huge group with varying flower sizes and colours. Largest are 'decoratives' with flat petals; cactus types have spiky, tubular flowers and pompons are rounded. Bedding series include 'Redskin' or 'Figaro'.
● Tubers must be lifted for safe overwintering.

DENDRANTHEMA Chrysanthemum
HP ○ ● ▨ ▨/⚘

30cm–1.2m/1–4ft. Ancient cultivated plants that produce flowers in all colours except blue. For bedding use, outdoor spray varieties such as pink 'Mei Kyo', 'Ruby Mound' or any of the Korean varieties are best.
● Best rooted from basal cuttings in winter but can be divided.

DIANTHUS Pink
HP ○ □ ❁ ▦/▨

To 30cm/1ft. Sun-loving plants with narrow foliage and fragrant flowers in clean, bright hues. Sweet williams (*D. barbatus*) are good bedders and come in dwarf series, such as 'Pinnochio Mixed', as well as taller varieties. Annual *Dianthus* series such as 'Baby Doll Mixed' or 'Snow Fire' are good for dwarf bedding schemes.
● Seed must be sown early to guarantee full flowering in late summer.

DORONICUM Leopard's Bane
HP ○/◐ ● ✻ ▨

15–45cm/6in–1½ft. Spring perennials grow to a height of 1m/3ft but most flower at around 45cm/1½ ft. 'Spring Beauty' is a dwarf with double blooms.
● Divide plants at least every two years.

ESCHSCHOLZIA
HA ○ □ ❁/▨ ▦

30cm/1ft. Easy annuals with bright orange, salmon or yellow blooms set off by glaucous filigree foliage. 'Dalli' has near-red blooms and 'Sundew' is creamy yellow.
● Sow outdoors in spring or allow plants to resow themselves at regular intervals. Select by pulling out unwanted colours as soon as the first flowers begin to appear.

FELICIA Kingfisher daisy
TP ○ ● ❁/▨ ▦/⚘

30cm/1ft. Lax-stemmed perennials with vivid blue daisy flowers, each with a golden centre. *F. amelloïdes* is one of the most popular, with the form 'Santa Anita' having the largest flowers. Good for containers.
● Cuttings root easily in late summer.

FUCHSIA
TS ○/◐ ● ❁/▨ ⚘

15cm–2m/6in–6ft. This is a vast group of shrubs with a wide range of uses from formal standards to hanging basket and window box plants. The plant bears pendulous flowers in pink, purple-blue and red shades and is perpetual flowering. Notable varieties include 'Thalia' with its thin, red blooms and dark foliage; the red and white 'Chequerboard'; and the redoubtable blue and red 'Mrs Popple'.
● Cuttings are easy to strike at any time during the growing season. Watch for red spider and vine weevil; both are scourges of the fuchsia and need to be promptly dealt with.

GAZANIA
TP grown as HHA ○ ● ❁ ⚘/▦

15cm/6in. Fine, lobed, silver foliage with startling flowers in warm tones. Seed series include 'Talent Mixed' and 'Ministar' but such cultivars as 'Cream Beauty' and *G. rigens* 'Variegata' are worth growing from cuttings or division.
● Sow seed under glass in late winter. Flowers best in a hot, sunny site.

GLECHOMA Ground Ivy
HP ○/✻ ● ✻/❁ ⚘/▨

8cm/3in, spreading several feet. This is a trailing plant, useful in its variegated form for growing in hanging baskets and containers. The foliage is grey-green in colour with cream markings, the flowers, though they are seldom seen, are small and blue. *G. hederacea* 'Variegata' is the only worthwhile variety.
● Easily rooted from divisions, but can be invasive if allowed to root in the ground.

HELICHRYSUM
TP/HA ○ ● ❁ ⚘/▦

To 30cm/1ft, trailing several feet. The silver-leaved, trailing *H. petiolare* is universally popular for containers. Coloured-leaf forms include the golden 'Limelight' and 'Variegatum'. *H plecostachys* also trails but with much smaller foliage.
● Pinch back when young in order to promote multiple shooting.

HYACINTHUS
B ○/◐ ● ✻ ▨

To 20cm/8in. Fragrant Dutch hyacinths make colourful spring displays in white, pink or blue. 'Myosotis', 'City of Haarlem' (cream) and 'Pink Pearl' all bed well.
● Planted deeply, they will flower for many years *in situ*.

IMPATIENS Busy Lizzie
TP grown as HHA ❁/✻ ● ❁ ▦/⚘

To 45cm/1½ft. Colourful, very vigorous plants in the balsam family, with soft, fleshy stems and endless, colourful flowers in pink, white, mauve or red shades. The 'Tempo' series is reliable, as are the 'Super Elfin' varieties. 'New Guinea' balsams are also good candidates for bedding schemes with their darker foliage.
● Seedlings need special care with watering soon after germinating, but are otherwise easy to raise. They dislike strong sun. Doubles and foliage kinds may only come true from cuttings.

IRESINE Beefsteak plant
TP ○ ● ❁ ⚘

To 60cm/2ft. *I. herbstii* and *I. lindenii* are both useful species with red foliage but insignificant flowers.
● Propagate from stem cuttings. Pinch back frequently when young.

LAMIUM Dead nettle
HP ○/◐ ● ✻/❁/▨/✻ ⚘/▦/▨

To 30cm/1ft, spreading. *L. maculatum* grows like a weed but is pretty with flower and foliage. Good cultivars include 'White Nancy' (silver foliage, white flowers) and 'Beacon Silver' (pink blooms).
● Easy to propagate by division at any time.

LATHYRUS Sweet Pea
HA ○ ● ❁ ▦

To 2.5m/8ft. Climber bearing fragrant blooms in most colours over a period of many months, especially if blooms are gathered regularly. Compact forms include 'Supersnoop' and the semi-dwarf 'Jet Set', both useful for growing in hanging baskets and containers. Tall kinds include the crimson 'Winston Churchill', 'White Ensign' and hundreds more.

LAVANDULA Lavender
HS ○ ● ◐/✿/✽ ♥/▦
30–60cm/1–2ft. Best bedding varieties include such compact forms as the deep purple 'Hidcote' and blue 'Munstead'.
● Simple to raise from cuttings. Prune hard after flowering to ensure healthy autumn foliage.

LAVATERA Annual mallow
HA ○ ● ✿ ♥/▦
30–60cm/1–2ft. Rapid-growing, easy annuals with clean-coloured, trumpet flowers all summer. Useful for bedding in windy conditions. Pink 'Silver Cup' and white 'Mont Blanc' are the most resilient.
● Sow indoors and plant out in late spring to achieve best results.

LIMNANTHES Poached Egg plant
HA ○/◐ ● ✄/✿ ▦
15cm/6in. Dwarf annual smothered, in early summer, with yellow and white blooms. Later, forms a carpet of self-sown young.

LOBELIA
TP grown as HHA ○/◐ ● ✿ ♥/▦
15cm/6in. The mainstay of most bedding, with trailing and dwarf forms in shades of blue, white or purple. Among seed-raised forms, 'Mrs Clibran Improved' has blue flowers with a white eye; 'Sapphire' is a trailing form and 'Rosamund' is cherry red. Perennial kinds, raised from cuttings or division, include 'Tim Rees' and the species, *L. erinus*.
● Fine seed: sow pinches of it in plugs. Take cuttings of perennial kinds.

LUNARIA Honesty
HB ◐/✽ ● ✄/✿ ▦
75cm/2½ft. Easily grown biennials with purple or white flowers and good seedheads. *L. annua* 'Alba Variegata' is especially good.
● Seedlings can be transplanted young for bedding, or sown directly.

MALCOLMIA Virginian Stock
HA ○ ● ✄/✿/◐ ▦
15cm/6in. Dwarf, fast and easy to grow. Tiny flowers in shades of pink, red, mauve and greenish white. Will self-sow in light, fertile soil to make a pretty cover.
● Sow at 4 week intervals for sustained displays.

MATTHIOLA Stock
HB ○ ● ✄/✿ ▦
30–60cm/1–2ft. The most fragrant of all bedding plants with blue-green foliage and flowers in pastel shades. 'Ten Week' stocks are best raised from seed under glass, planted out in spring. 'Brompton' stocks are sown outdoors in summer to flower in spring, in mild areas.
● In some strains, double forms can be selected out at seedling stage.

MAURANDYA (Syn. *Asalina*)
TP ○ ● ✿ ▦
1–1.2m/3–4ft. Herbaceous climbers which need frost protection. The flowers are trumpet-shaped. Species include *A. barclaiana* (blue to purple) and *A. erubescens* (pink).
● Raise from spring-sown seed which has been started under glass.

MESEMBRYANTHEMUM Livingstone Daisy
HHA ○ ● ✿ ▦
15cm/6in. Mixtures include 'Magic Carpet' or 'Sparkles' but 'Lunette' has soft, yellow blooms.
● Needs full sun to flower well. Protect young seedlings from slugs.

MIMULUS Musk
HP grown as HHA ○/◐ ≋ ✿ ▦/♥/◼
15–30cm/6in–2ft. Produces pansy-like flowers over long periods in yellow, gold and scarlet hues. Seed series such as 'Calypso' offer a wide, jazzy colour range but 'Andean Nymph', a subtle pastel combination of creams, pinks and speckles, and *M. cupreus* 'Red Emperor' are smaller and classier.

MUSCARI Grape hyacinth
B ○ ● ✄ ◼
10–20cm/4–8in. Vivid blue flowers in spring, creating a striking carpet when massed. 'Blue Spike' and 'Plumosum' are dependable; *M. botryoides* 'Album' is a pretty white.
● Plant out in autumn, 10cm/4in deep, for spring flowering.

NARCISSUS Jonquil, daffodil
B ✽/◐ ● ✄ ◼
10–45cm/4in–1½ft. Daffodils, jonquils and narcissus are in this most popular range. 'February Gold' is early; 'Pheasant Eye' is the late 'poet's narcissus', but there are hundreds more.
● Most prefer deep planting in good soil. Do not cut back foliage until at least six weeks after flowering has ended.

NEMESIA
HHA ○ ● ✄/✿ ▦
To 30cm/1ft. Distinctive flowers in warm colours, less long-lived than some bedding. Mixes include 'Carnival' (bright) and 'Pastel' (softer shades) but 'Mello Red' and 'Mellow White' are fine, self-coloured series.
● Raise from seed sown in late winter in gentle heat. Fertile soil guarantees longer flowering.

NICOTIANA Tobacco Plant
TP grown as HHA ○ ● ✿ ▦
20–60cm/8in–2ft or more. A bedding mainstay with trumpet flowers and felty, sticky foliage. Flowers of *N. affinis* wilt by day but perk up and exude fragrance at night. New varieties include the compact and floriferous 'Domino' series. Species like *N. sylvestris* (white) and *N. langsdorffii* (green) are also splendid.
● Bedding forms are raised from seed sown in spring under glass. Sow *N. sylvestris* indoors in winter to ensure large plants.

NIGELLA Love-in-a-Mist
HA ○ ● ✿ ▦
30cm/1ft. Misty foliage and blue flowers. 'Miss Jekyll' (mid-blue) is a fine old variety, but 'Persian Jewels' provides mixed colour.
● Best direct sown and thinned to 20cm/8in apart. Will self-seed in permanent plantings.

OSTEOSPERMUM
TP/HP ○ ▢ ✿ ♥/▦
30–60cm/1–2ft. Daisy-like, pale-faced blooms open to the sun; petal backs are darker. 'Buttermilk' is buffish primrose; 'Whirligig' has odd-shaped flowers; 'Silver Sparkler' has variegated leaves.
● Feed and deadhead to keep in flower.

PAPAVER Poppy
HA ☼ ● ❀ ▨

20cm–1m/8in–3ft. 'Shirley' poppies make fine bedding in pink, lemon and white. *P. somniferum* has glaucous foliage.
● Direct sow outdoors in early spring or, in mild areas, in autumn.

PELARGONIUM Pot Geranium
TP ☼ ● ❀/⊘ ⚘/▨

15cm–1m/6in–3ft or more. Vast range of bedding plants. As well as Regal pelargoniums and scented-leaf kinds, the two most important groups are as follows:
Zonal pelargoniums: Traditional pot geraniums including seed strains such as 'Multibloom' or 'Orbit' series and named cultivars such as the variegated 'Frank Headley' and the dwarf red 'Friesdorf'. All prefer fertile soil in full sun.
Pelargonium peltatum: Ivy-leaved, trailing forms, perfect for containers, including the scarlet 'Balcon Royale', variegated 'L'Elegante' and the brooding 'Barbe Bleu'. Pinch back repeatedly in early season to thicken growth.
● All are easily grown from cuttings. Seed-raised forms are best sown in late winter to ensure large plants for bedding out. Pelargoniums are easy to overwinter in a dormant state. Lift plants in autumn and store, almost dry, in a cool but frost-free place.

PENSTEMON
TP/HP ☼ ● ❀ ⚘/▨

To 1m/3ft. Easy perennials with tubular flowers in many colours. 'Evelyn' (pink) and 'Firebird' are hardy hybrids. The mauve 'Alice Hindley' is more tender.
● Strike cuttings in autumn for spring flowering. Cut regularly to prolong flowering period.

PETUNIA
TP ☼ ●/□ ❀ ⚘/▨

20–45cm/8in–1½ft. Felty, trumpet flowers available in almost every colour. Current favourites include 'Frenzy' series and the large-flowered F1 'Falcon' range. Trailing kinds such as 'Surfina' are the latest craze. New series frequently introduced.
● Seed is very fine, sow with care.

PHLOX
HHA/HP ☼ ● ❀ ▨/◿

15–30cm/6in–1ft. Annual form, *Phlox drummondii*, is best for bedding. Dwarf forms include 'Fantasy', but there are frilled flower kinds such as 'Twinkle'.
● Sow seed under glass. Plant in fertile soil in full sun. Susceptible to slug damage when young.

PLECTRANTHUS
TP ☼/◑ ● ❀ ⚘

10cm/4in high, spreading several feet. *P. forsteri* is a variegated trailing plant, useful as 'backing' in hanging baskets or containers.
● Growing stems pushed gently into the compost and pegged down will root to create new plants.

PORTULACA
HHA ☼ ●/□ ❀ ▨

10–20cm/4–8in. These are low growing succulents with flowers in shades of red, pink, cream and yellow. 'Sundial' offers a good colour range; 'Cloudbeater' has double flowers that stay open in dull weather.
● Sow in gentle heat in late winter. Prone to damping off: do not over-water.

PRIMULA Primrose, Polyanthus
HP ❀/✦ ● ✗ ▨/◿

10–30cm/4in–1ft. A mainstay of spring bedding. Polyanthus series include 'Crescendo' (huge flowers) and 'Cowichan' in sombre shades. Primrose series include 'Wanda Hybrids' with dark foliage, and 'Juliana Mini-Hybrids' with starred flowers. Drumstick primulas (*P. denticulata*) are fine for bedding in areas of damp soil.
● Protect from bird damage by suspending threads over plants. Divide plants after flowering to keep them young.

RICINUS Castor Oil Plant
TP ☼ ● ❀ ▨

To 2m/6ft. A dot plant. Usually grown as an annual for its big palmate leaves. Showy seed capsules. 'Impala' has reddened leaves. This plant is poisonous.
● Copious feeding and rapid growth without check will guarantee large, well-coloured leaves and strong plants.

RUDBECKIA Cone Flower
HP/HA ☼ ● ❀/⊘ ▨/◿

20cm–1m/8in–3ft. Bold, rayed flowers in warm oranges, golds and tortoiseshell. 'Marmalade' is a dependable tall favourite; dwarf series include 'Becky'. Perennial forms such as 'Goldsturm' also bed well.
● Sow in midwinter or spring under glass. Transplant divisions of perennial kinds the preceding autumn.

SALPIGLOSSIS
HHA ☼ ● ❀ ▨

To 60cm/2ft. Veined, trumpet flowers which resemble petunias and tobacco plants, to which they are related. 'Splash' series grow tall but F2 'Bolero' are more compact.
● Sow in spring with heat, but do not plant outdoors too early.

SALVIA
TP/HP/HHA ☼ ●/≋ ❀/⊘ ⚘/▨/◿

15cm–2m/6in–6ft. Huge genus with many useful species. Tender salvias include *S. coccinea* (red) and *S. involucrata* 'Bethellii' (pink), both can be raised from cuttings; bedding kinds such as *S. splendens* (red) and *S. farinacea* 'Victoria' (blue) are seed raised.
● Most salvias prefer good growing conditions with moist soil, but plenty of sunshine.

SANTOLINA Cotton lavender
HS ☼ ●/□ ❀/⊘/✳ ⚘

15–45cm/6in–1½ft. Silver foliage, yellow button flowers. An alternative to lavender for low hedging or carpeting. *S. neapolitana* has silvery foliage, *S. rosmarinifolia* is green.
● The flowers should be removed as soon as they fade and bushes clipped back to foster new growth.

SENECIO
TP/HP ☼ ● ❀ ⚘/▨

30cm–1m/1–3ft. Good foliage plants. *S. viravira* and *S. cineraria* have silver foliage which provides an attractive background for bedding schemes. Seed strains include 'Silver Dust'.
● Almost hardy but easiest sown under glass and planted out.

TAGETES Marigold
HHA ○ ● ✿ ※
15–60cm/6in–2ft. Among the brightest bedders with rank-smelling foliage and ruffled flowers in yellows and oranges. Tall African marigolds include F1 'Discovery' series; shorter French marigolds include 'Bonita Mixed' and, for a single flowered kind, try 'Naughty Marietta'.
● Among the easiest plants. Sow in spring in heat, plant out in full sunshine in good soil.

TANACETUM (Matricaria) Feverfew
HP ○ ● ✿ ♣/※
15cm–1m/6in–3ft. Aromatic members of the aster family with button-like flowers. T. parthenium is useful as foliage, especially in its golden form. Seed series include 'Butterball' and 'Sanata Lemon'.
● Easy to grow but best regularly pinched back. Watch out for self-seeding as some forms can be invasive.

THYMUS Thyme
HP ○ ● ✿ ♣/※/◪
15cm/6in. Evergreen aromatic herbs with small leaves, handy as bordering material. Variegated forms like 'Silver Posy' or 'Nyewood' make pretty alternatives to green-leaved thymes. All have pinkish purple (or, occasionally, white) flowers.
● Keep trimmed to encourage new growth.

TITHONIA Mexican Sunflower
HHA ○ ● ✿ ※
75cm/2½ft. Vivid orange blooms set off by emerald foliage.
● Sow seed in late winter under glass. Must be deadheaded regularly to promote free flowering.

TOLMIEA Piggy-back plant
HP ◑/✳ ● ✖/✿/∅ ♣/◪
20–30cm/8in–1ft. T. menziesii 'Taff's Gold' forms low mats of marbled foliage. Excellent in hanging baskets.
● Easily multiplied by pulling away new shoots from leaf centres and re-planting.

TROPAEOLUM Nasturtium
TP/HP/HA ○ ● ✿ ※
20cm/8in, some trailing to several feet. Main bedding species is the trailing T. majus. Compact forms include 'Empress of India' (crimson) and 'Strawberries and Cream'. 'Alaska' has marbled foliage, 'Climbing Mixed' is more vigorous.

TULIPA
B ○ ● ✖ ◪
15–75cm/6in–2½ft. T. fosteriana 'White Emperor' is a huge-flowered early form; 'Apeldoorn' (red) plus all its colour sports (yellow, orange) is the perfect midseason tulip; soft, pink 'Clara Butt' is a fine, late 'Cottage' variety.
● Bulbs should be planted at least 15cm/6in deep for best results.

VERBENA
TP/HP grown as HHA ○ ●/□ ✿/∅ ♣/※
30cm/1ft. Creeping rootstock enables the plants to form colourful mats with flowers in bright umbels. 'Sissinghurst' (pink) is one of the finest spreaders but new varieties such as the soft-coloured 'Peaches and Cream' show great promise.
● Can be easily grown from seed or can be raised from cuttings taken in autumn and over-wintered under glass.

VIOLA Pansy, violet
HP/HA ○/◑ ● ✖/✿/∅/✳ ♣/※/◪
8–30cm/3in–1ft. Huge groups occupy this genus from tiny violets to giant pansies. Of the winter pansies, the 'Universal' series is best for winter and spring. 'General purpose' varieties such as 'Maggie Mott' and 'Irish Molly' are long-lived perennials, while the blue or white V. cornuta flowers almost constantly.
● Pansy seed needs low temperatures in order for it to germinate. Trim back growth frequently to avoid legginess, and deadhead plants as often as possible.

ZINNIA
HHA ○ ● ✿ ※
20cm–1m/8in–3ft. Brilliant flowers, rather like dahlias, that need warm conditions and plenty of sun to flower. Dwarf kinds such as 'Persian carpet' or 'Whirligig' mix (30cm/1ft) often do better in cool areas.
Sow seed under protection in spring. Watch for slug damage.

Index

Note: Page numbers in *italic* indicate illustrations. For reasons of space, page references to the Plant Directory (pages 88-93), which gives specific cultivation notes and guidance on plant varieties, are not included in this Index.

ACKNOWLEDGMENTS

The publishers would like to thank the following photographers and organisations for their kind permission to reproduce the photographs in this book:

1 Clive Nichols; 2-3 Didier Willery/Garden Picture Library; 6-7 S&O Mathews; 7 Andrew Lawson; 8 Annette Schreiner; 9 S&O Mathews; 10 John Glover; 11 Clive Nichols (40 Osler Road, Oxford); 16 Jerry Harpur (Fudlers Hall, Chelmsford); 17 above Clive Nichols (Lygon Arms Hotel, Broadway Village, Hereford & Worcester); 17 below Michele Lamontagne; 18 (background) Brian Carter/Garden Picture Library; 19 left John Glover; 19 right (background) Brian Carter/Garden Picture Library; 20-21 Brigitte Perdereau; 21 right Brigitte Perdereau; 22 left Michele Lamontagne; 22-23 Jerry Harpur (Longwood, Philadelphia); 24 Andrew Lawson; 25 John Glover; 28 Michele Lamontagne; 29 above S&O Mathews; 29 below Brigitte Perdereau; 30 J.S. Sira/Garden Picture Library; 31 Tim Sandall; 32-33 S&O Mathews; 33 right Patrick McLeavey; 34 Michele Lamontagne; 35 John Glover; 36 (background strip) Photos Horticultural; 37 (background strips) Photos Horticultural; 38 Derek Gould; 39 above Andrew Lawson; 42 left Tim Sandall; 42 right Tim Sandall; 43 above left Tim Sandall; 43 above right Tim Sandall; 43 below Tim Sandall; 44 Clive Nichols (Chenies Manor, Bucks); 46-47 Clive Nichols (Waterperry Gardens, Oxfordshire); 47 right Clive Nichols (Chenies Manor, Bucks); 48 Michele Lamontagne; 49 John Glover; 50 left (background) Patrick McLeavey; 50 right Jerry Harpur (RHS Wisley); 51 Clive Nichols; 52 left Jerry Harpur (La Mamounia, Marrakech); 52-53 Brigitte Perdereau; 53 right Linda Burgess/Garden Picture Library; 54 above Brigitte Perdereau; 54 below S&O Mathews; 55 left Annette Schreiner; 55 right (background) Patrick McLeavey; 58 left (background) Andrew Lawson; 58 right Michele Lamontagne; 59 above Densey Clyne/Garden Picture Library; 59 below S&O Mathews; 60 Jerry Harpur (Designer: Claus Schreinert, La Casella); 61 above left Hugh Palmer; 61 below left Patrick McLeavey; 61 right (background) Andrew Lawson; 64-65 Clive Nichols (Tintinhull House Garden, Somerset); 65 right Andrew Lawson; 66 Brigitte Perdereau; 67 left Clive Nichols (Greencombe Garden, Somerset); 67 right (background) Brigitte Perdereau; 68 Derek Gould; 69 Clive Nichols (Chenies Manor, Bucks.); 70 left (background) Patrick McLeavey; 70 above right Hugh Palmer; 70 below right Clive Nichols (Old Court Nurseries, Hereford & Worcester); 71 Jacqui Hurst; 72 left (background) Michele Lamontagne; 72 right Annette

Schriener; 73 Hugh Palmer; 74 Annette Schreiner; 75 left Photos Horticultural; 75 centre Michele Lamontagne; 75 right (background) Michele Lamontagne; 76 Andrew Lawson; 77 above S&O Mathews; 77 below Hugh Palmer; 80 (background) Photos Horticultural; 81 above Brigitte Perdereau; 81 below Michele Lamontagne; 82 Clive Nichols (Keukenhof Gardens, Holland); 83 Brigitte Perdereau; 84 left (background) Brian Carter/Garden Picture Library; 84 right S&O Mathews; 85 above Michele Lamontagne; 85 below Brian Carter/Garden Picture Library; 86 left (background) Brian Carter/Garden Picture Library; 86 above centre Michele Lamontagne; 86 below centre Derek Gould; 86-87 Vaughan Fleming/Garden Picture Library; 87 right (background) Brian Carter/Garden Picture Library.

The following photographs were specially taken for Conran Octopus by Clive Nichols in Nigel Colborn's garden: 4-5, 12, 13, 14, 15, 26, 27, 36 left, 36 centre, 36 right, 37 above left, 37 above centre, 37 above right, 37 below right, 39 below left, 39 below centre, 39 below right, 40, 41, 56, 57, 62, 63, 65, 78, 79.

The publishers would also like to thank Chris Blom of Walter Blom & Sons Ltd and Elizabeth Macleod Matthews for plant naming on page 68.

Author's acknowledgments

My grateful thanks to seedsmen, Thompson and Morgan, for their help in providing seed varieties, and especially to Janie Pirie and Keith Sangster. Also to Brian Salter of Robinson's, Winchester, in whose greenhouses many of my best plants have been raised.

Thanks also to those gardening friends who champion annuals and bedding plants; in particular Graham Rice, whose plant knowledge is profound, Brian Halliwell who, at Kew, showed how imaginative bedding could be and Helen Robinson, who revived my interest in such precious garden genera as *Pelargonium* and *Fuchsia*.

Thanks also to my father, Leslie Colborn, not only for giving me trays of home-raised seedlings for this project, but also for having shown me, as a small boy long ago, how to prick them out and grow them on!